S
D

Published by
Princeton Architectural Press
202 Warren Street
Hudson, New York 12534

Visit our website at www.papress.com.

Cover image: architect: Oppenheim Architecture + Design; rendering: Dbox

Editor: Laurie Manfra and Megan Carey
Designer: Jan Haux

Special thanks to: Bree Anne Apperley, Sara Bader, Nicholas Beatty,
Nicola Bednarek Brower, Janet Behning, Fannie Bushin, Carina Cha,
Russell Fernandez, Linda Lee, Diane Levinson, Jennifer Lippert,
Gina Morrow, John Myers, Katharine Myers, Margaret Rogalski,
Dan Simon, Sara Stemen, Andrew Stepanian, Paul Wagner, and
Joseph Weston of Princeton Architectural Press
—Kevin C. Lippert, publisher

Library of Congress Cataloging-in-Publication Data
Bergman, David, 1956–
 Sustainable design : a critical guide. / David Bergman. — 1st ed.
144 pages : illustrations (chiefly color) ; 22 cm. — (Architecture briefs series)
 Includes bibliographical references.
 ISBN 978-1-56898-941-9 (alk. paper)
 1. Sustainable design. 2. Sustainable architecture. I. Title. II. Title: Critical
guide.
 NK1520.B48 2011
 720'.47—dc22
                                    2011010528

Sustainable Design

A Critical Guide

David Bergman

Princeton Architectural Press, New York

The **Architecture Briefs** series takes on a variety of single topics of interest to architecture students and young professionals. Field-specific and technical information are presented in a user-friendly manner along with basic principles of design and construction. The series familiarizes readers with the concepts and technical terms necessary to successfully translate ideas into built form.

Also in this series:

Architects Draw
Sue Ferguson Gussow / 978-1-56898-740-8

Architectural Lighting: Designing with Light and Space
Hervé Descottes and Cecilia E. Ramos / 978-1-56898-938-9

Architectural Photography the Digital Way
Gerry Kopelow / 978-1-56898-697-5

Building Envelopes: An Integrated Approach
Jenny Lovell / 978-1-56898-818-4

Digital Fabrications: Architectural and Material Techniques
Lisa Iwamoto / 978-1-56898-790-3

Ethics for Architects: 50 Dilemmas of Professional Practice
Thomas Fisher / 978-1-56898-946-4

Material Strategies: Innovative Applications in Architecture
Blaine Brownell / 978-1-56898-986-0

Model Making
Megan Werner / 978-1-56898-870-2

Old Buildings, New Designs: Architectural Transformations
Charles Bloszies / 978-1-61689-035-3

Philosophy for Architects
Branko Mitrović / 978-1-56898-994-5

Urban Composition: Developing Community through Design
Mark C. Childs / 978-1-61689-052-0

Writing about Architecture: Mastering the Language of Buildings and Cities
Alexandra Lange / 978-1-61689-053-7

Contents

Acknowledgments

It would risk extreme hubris to start without acknowledging the vast body of preceding work by others, which I've attempted to synthesize and organize into this brief. Often, it is by people I have never met but whose writings or designs I have admired, learned from, and perhaps incorporated here. These are the people who laid the groundwork for contemporary environmentalism and sustainable design, people who predate the bandwagon, from Thoreau and his fears of future technology to Bucky Fuller and his ardent visions of technological solutions, from the forebodings of Rachel Carson to the tentative optimism of Bill McKibben and the exuberant designs emerging worldwide.

Of course, there is also a long list of people I need to thank specifically. First must be Kevin Lippert, who approached me to write this book. Also at Princeton Architectural Press: Clare Jacobson, Laurie Manfra, Jennifer Lippert, and especially Jan Haux and Megan Carey.

Thank you to my extremely helpful and resourceful assistants, Jason Bailey and Michelle Carrieri. Michael Bogdanffy-Kreigh, David K. Sargert, and Chris Garvin provided much valued input for the early versions of the manuscript. I undoubtedly have left some names off the following list of those who directly or indirectly provided assistance and encouragement: Alan Abrams, Amelia Amon, Dan Blitzer, Wendy Brawer, Erika Doering, Josh Dorfman, Manny Feris, John Ferry, Paul Goldberger, Lori Ito Hardenbergh, Alice Hartley, Mitchell Joaquim, Ellen Dunham-Jones, Cathy Kaufman, Tim Vireo Keating, Wilder Knight, Alexis Kraft, Conor Lally, Chandler Lee, Nadav Malin, Anne Mandelbaum, Michael Mandelbaum, Paul S. Mankiewicz, Mark Osmun, Walter Pearce, Philip Proefrock, Jeremy Shannon, Lenny Stein, Susan Szenasy, Cameron Tonkinwise, and David White.

Teaching at Parsons The New School for Design and elsewhere has provided me with the continuing impetus to find coherent and succinct ways to explain concepts that are often complex and overlapping. For starting me on that path, I owe major gratitude to Tony Whitfield.

I'd like to think I gleaned from my father, Jules Bergman, the importance of distilling those complex concepts into comprehensible bits of understanding that can be reassembled to better explain the whole. Among his television science reports, he covered—and made accessible to the nontechnical viewer—early environmental topics such as solar power, asbestos, and clear-cutting.

The influence of my mother, Joanne Bergman, ranged from providing me with every building toy known to 1960s western civilization to engaging me in early environmentalism. I recall being volunteered for activities like trudging through muddy local forests to survey the wetlands remaining between the pre-McMansion subdivisions. (Or did I volunteer her?) Only recently did I figure out that who I am is no accident.

And the proverbial last-but-certainly-not-least is my wife and CEE Lori Greenberg. Years ago, a magazine editor asked us what Lori's position at my product design company was and I flippantly replied Chief of Everything Else. For this book, Lori was art director and primary shoulder. That doesn't begin to sum up what this book and I owe her.

Introduction

Let's clear the air (so to speak) right away. This is not a book about doom and gloom. We won't spend a lot of time talking about environmental crises. Many others have taken care of that, and whether or not you believe that climate change is the upcoming apocalypse—it's actually not the only environmental concern we face—we don't need to dwell on it. The rationales for ecodesign reach far beyond the singular goal of mitigating climate change to include setting the stage for the future—the sustaining—of our species and aspiring still further to a positive outcome: improving the quality of our lives.

Too often environmentalists take the view that we have been bad and must amend our ways, that sacrifice is the necessary path, that we have been irresponsible and we have to give up modern comforts to become more responsible. That approach is not going to work. Most of us have grown used to our ways, and it would be impossible to turn back the clock to how we lived before the Industrial Revolution. Doom-and-gloomists (who are more likely to call themselves realists) would say we have no choice: the dual problems of consumption and population cannot be overcome any other way. But sacrifice does not represent a desirable path or one that most of us would undertake voluntarily. Furthermore, getting rid of technology and modern comforts will not solve our problems. Take cars, for example. The back-to-our-roots approach, which some people consider environmentalism to be, would have us trade in cars for horses. But I doubt we'd like manure-filled streets any more than we like greenhouse gases and traffic jams. The same is true for other areas of technology: reverting from electric or gas furnaces to wood-burning fireplaces on a widespread level is worse environmentally.

We don't need to go backward. There are plenty of design paths, some shovel-ready and others on the near horizon, that will allow us to live comfortably (maybe even more so) within the means of our incredible planet. This isn't the same as saying that we don't need to change or rethink our lifestyles. We certainly do, and that, many argue, will lead to improvements in our lives.

Technology can provide both realistic and unrealistic solutions. Buckminster Fuller's dome over midtown Manhattan for climate control was one of his more unrealistic solutions.

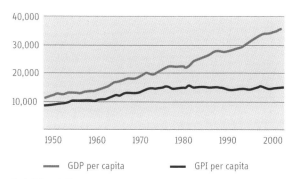

Real GDP and GPI per capita, 1950–2004, adjusted for inflation (adapted from Redefining Progress).

Many of the choices we appear to face take the form of false dichotomies, either-or dilemmas for which the possibility of other solutions is overlooked. The alternative to a car-dependent society is not horses alone. Choosing between bad and worse heating systems is less of a problem if our buildings are designed to need less heating in the first place.

Another approach posits that since technology got us into this situation, it will get us out of it. As the popular analogy goes, If we can put a man on the moon.... In the chapters that follow, you'll see a lot of technological fixes; but you'll also encounter other kinds of solutions, involving social and individual choices that reevaluate how we want to live our lives, what we value, and how we derive satisfaction and happiness.

Note that latter point: how we derive happiness. While the pressing need is to design and build in ways that better sustain the natural environment, our objective is not just to stop biting the hand that feeds us, but also to bandage and heal that hand while improving our lives. That's very far from doom and gloom and the notion that the only viable path is one of self-sacrifice. In fact, we can make the world a better place both ecologically and anthropogenically, that is, from the points of view of the Earth and humanity. Actually, the two are inseparable. Our interests are one and the same. In spite of all our technology, we need the Earth's ecosystems in order to survive. We might be able to think and invent our way out of problems like rising sea levels or a scarcity of fresh water, but it will be much more difficult and expensive and cause greater human suffering than if we work with, instead of against, nature's systems.

Our objective as a profession is to create designs for the built world that not only conserve the environment, but also preserve and enhance the lives of everyone: symbiotic solutions. I don't mean to suggest that these solutions won't require changes to our lives: there's no getting around the fact that we (especially in the Western world) are consuming resources at an insatiable rate. But change does not have to equal sacrifice. We can and should consume less, and we can do so without diminishing our quality of life.

We'll discuss many win-win (and often win-win-win) solutions in the chapters ahead. The term I propose for this way of thinking, which assumes that we have the potential to come out of this predicament for the better, is *eco-optimism*. It's the opposite of how one might have felt after seeing *An Inconvenient Truth*. (I once attended a screening of another ecodocumentary that was so profoundly depressing that everyone in the theater headed straight for the nearest bar afterward.) To paraphrase an *X-Files* line, the solutions are out there. We just have to implement them.

The concepts and solutions in the following pages fall into two categories. The first involves incremental steps, or what I call tweaks: things like adding insulation, using low-flow toilets, or switching to compact fluorescent lights. Such important solutions are often inexpensive and worthwhile (the low-hanging fruit) and found by applying the basic three Rs of environmentalism: reduce, reuse, and recycle.

The second category is what some call the fourth R: rethink. Related to the discussion of false dichotomies, rethinking usually involves taking a step back (which is not the same as going backward) to ask ourselves what we are trying to accomplish. For example, instead of asking how to make a cleaner, more energy-efficient lawn mower, we could ask if there is a better way to design the landscapes surrounding our buildings and infrastructure than planting water- and nutrient-dependent grasses. Rather than incorporating energy-efficient but expensive or complex heating and cooling systems, we could design buildings that rely less heavily on these systems or not at all. When we change how we ask the questions, the possibility of arriving at other answers emerges. These are the game changers, the concepts that have the potential both to alleviate environmental concerns and to improve our lives, and they come with an architectural bonus. They also offer the most interesting design possibilities, because they represent fertile new territory.

Ecodesign is the opportunity to go far beyond tweaks to develop new concepts and typologies, such as this structure at Nanyang Technological University's School of Art, Design & Media (2006) in Singapore, designed by CPG Consultants.

Tweaks are vital, especially as interim solutions; cumulatively, they can add up to a significant impact. Aesthetically, however, they are just the nuts and bolts of sustainable design, necessary but not fulfilling. For those who have chosen the design profession for its creative nature, the best possible solutions will synthesize a variety of tweaks with an ability to envision the future.

It's a challenge to define and explain sustainable architecture in the limited space of these pages. Rather than squeeze in every type of sustainable design, construction method, and material, I have attempted to discuss the essential components of ecodesign through specific materials and methods. Regard this Architecture Brief as a primer in sustainable architecture and design, defined as inclusively as possible. Some topics—for example, alternative construction systems like straw bale or rammed earth—have not been included, as interesting as they are. But the concepts underlying them—thermal mass, natural materials—are reviewed.

There are also areas of debate as to best solutions. In these instances, I have pointed out the viewpoints, the pros and cons, rather than prescribe a single answer where there may be none. Frequently, these viewpoints are evolving. As our expertise in sustainable design grows, knowledge is upended. Today's high-tech answer may contain issues yet to be realized. (For a historical example, see the discussion of tight buildings in chapter six, "Indoor Environmental Quality.")

In light of an evolving discipline, this book is intended as a guide, a base that organizes and explains the concepts and goals of sustainable design, and creates a jumping-off point from which those concepts can be further developed and physically emerge. In the ongoing maturation of ecodesign and its merger with the larger enterprise of design, this is a beginning, not an end.

Ecodesign: What and Why

As designers we have a divided set of responsibilities. Professionally and contractually, our primary obligation is to our clients, including a mandate to protect public safety. Artistically and financially, we also have certain obligations to ourselves. Beyond these, though, we have a duty to the public in a larger sense than the safety issues that licensing addresses. That ethical responsibility, which considers how our built designs affect the world, is both professional and personal.

One way to view this is to interpret public safety as encompassing environmental issues, for without the support of the Earth's ecosystems, human life would be threatened. We could not survive without the air, water, and atmospheric protection that our exquisitely tuned planet provides. Our lifestyles, if not our lives, are reliant on the "free" ecological services—oxygen creation, water filtration, nitrogen fixation, etc.—that we too often take for granted. It is by no means a leap, then, to say that a primary responsibility of designers is to protect—to sustain—these vital resources.

It's become a truism that green design is a valuable and necessary goal. But it's worth taking a few moments to establish just how important it is, before getting to *what* it is. Buildings are not the only cause of ecological issues. Blame can be shared with population growth, transportation, industrial agriculture, carnivorous diets, and our sometimes irrational desire for ever more stuff. How important are buildings in this gathering storm?

In 2003, Edward Mazria, who was a green architect before such a category existed, looked closely at the statistics of energy consumption in the United States and concluded that the role of buildings was far greater than expected, amounting to 48 percent of U.S. energy consumption and 46 percent of U.S. carbon dioxide production.[1] These statistics convey a significant point: climate change and other environmental issues are not someone else's problem; they are ours. They are not issues to be passed off to the worlds of government and business, though they, too, bear a large part of the responsibility. Buildings are our creations, and with that comes the need not only

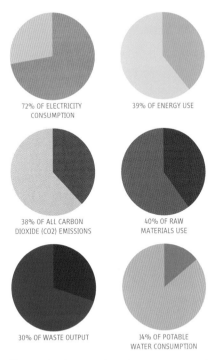

72% OF ELECTRICITY CONSUMPTION

39% OF ENERGY USE

38% OF ALL CARBON DIOXIDE (CO2) EMISSIONS

40% OF RAW MATERIALS USE

30% OF WASTE OUTPUT

14% OF POTABLE WATER CONSUMPTION

Diagram showing percentage of resources consumed by buildings alone (adapted from USGBC).

to make them durable, functional, and good-looking, but also to ensure that they are good citizens.

Mazria's numbers were eye-opening for the architecture and design community, sparking renewed concern over the role of buildings in our energy usage and dependence. Shortly thereafter, the film *An Inconvenient Truth* drew further attention to these issues. In the process, though, other no-less-important environmental issues—such as water pollution and usage, resource consumption, the effects of toxic materials, and social and ethical dilemmas—have sometimes been de-emphasized. While energy conservation and alternative energy development are indeed critical, a more holistic approach to design and construction is needed. The more encompassing objective is to ensure the well-being of our communities and the ecosystems that surround them for current and future generations.

And when we adopt this broader vision, we can begin to look anew at additional questions, asking what the role of a building is or should be. We tend to view buildings as discrete, independent objects inserted on the planet. A holistic view would see them as systems both unto themselves and inseparably tied to surrounding ecosystems.

Redefining the role of buildings and our relationships to them can take us in new directions artistically (what does an ecobuilding look like?) and beyond if we are modifying the goals of design to change what it is designers do.

The Beginnings of Green Design

What do we actually mean when we talk about green design, sustainable design, or ecodesign? Generally speaking, we can apply these terms interchangeably. While there may be nuanced differences between them, I find it more helpful to think in terms of what we are trying to achieve.

Ecodesign has evolved considerably from its 1960s origins, captured in the phrase "Reduce, reuse, recycle." The catchiness of the now ubiquitous three Rs helped immensely in expanding awareness, but that same simple edict has led some people to conclude that once they've recycled their bottles and newspapers and converted a lightbulb or two, they've done their part.

Similarly, designers who have included three R–type thinking, which can be thought of as the first level of ecodesign, may feel that their jobs are done. These are the tweaks described earlier, incremental changes that, while positive in general, do not go far enough because their goals are too limited or because they look at issues in isolation instead of holistically.

Cradle to Grave

To get beyond this crucial but narrow starting point, the concept of ecodesign has to be broadened. The first step in achieving this is to look at what is called, somewhat inaccurately, the life cycle of buildings and materials. Life cycle analysis (LCA), also known as life cycle assessment, has been applied more frequently to products, but the principles also apply to buildings.[2] The life of the product (or building) is examined from cradle to grave; that is, from the origin of its raw materials to the manipulation of these materials during manufacturing, to the consumption of energy and resources during its useful life, to the impact of its eventual end of life.

At each phase of the life cycle, there are material and energy inputs and corresponding environmental impacts. An LCA attempts to quantify all of these inputs and then come up with values to represent their impact. By analyzing the results of an LCA, a designer can evaluate where to improve or modify a creation; is it, for instance, more beneficial to increase energy efficiency, replace toxic materials, or convert to recycled materials?

The cradle-to-grave approach, while more encompassing than the three Rs, still has limitations. The use of the word *grave* implies that buildings and products have a linear life span. In this sense, life *cycle* analysis is a bit of a misnomer. Another shortcoming, in the words of ecodesign advocates Bill McDonough and Michael Braungart, is that the cradle-to-grave approach amounts merely to "being less bad." It enables us to see and reduce the overall impact of what we build, but it does not get us to the goal of sustainability.

Materials Acquisition

↓

Manufacturing

↓

Construction

↓

Occupancy

↓

Demolition

The cradle-to-grave life "cycle" of a building.

Cradle to Cradle

Putting the *cycle* back into life cycle analysis is the next conceptual leap we must make. This represents an expansion from cradle-to-grave to cradle-to-cradle thinking. Though this idea was popularized by McDonough and Braungart in their book *Cradle to Cradle: Remaking the Way We Make Things*, it has deeper roots, perhaps originating with Buckminster Fuller's *Operating Manual for Spaceship Earth*, in which Fuller compares the Earth to a spaceship starting its journey with a finite amount of resources that cannot be resupplied.[3] This concept was driven home in 1968 by the iconic image from Apollo 8 of our planet isolated in space. With that photograph in mind, pondering how we make things and where the materials come from will quickly lead to a visceral grasp of Fuller's prescient point. Our materials (iron, coal, oil, agricultural nutrients, etc.), as well as the air and water we require for life, do not get replenished from outside the Earth's closed system floating through the universe. Everything we have and ever will have is, in one form or another, on the planet now. (Given the tremendous cost and energy requirement of spaceflight, we are unlikely ever to bring back useful quantities of materials from other planets.) Therefore, to be truly sustainable, we must never use up resources faster than the Earth's ecosystems can replenish them.

However, there is one critical exception. Because solar energy is constantly replenished, falling on the Earth every day, we can use it without fear of running out. This includes energy derived directly from sunlight, as well as related renewable sources, such as wind and biofuels, that would not exist without the presence of the sun and, by loose extension, tidal and geothermal energies.[4]

Prior to humanity's presence, the Earth existed with the fundamental constraints of a finite system for eons and therefore developed ingenious systems in which nothing is ever discarded. If it had not, some resources would have been exhausted over time. But nature is an expert at efficiency and symbiosis and long ago demonstrated a concept that we verbalized only recently: waste = food. This

Buckminster Fuller's *Operating Manual for Spaceship Earth*.

All materials should be considered to exist either in a biological nutrient cycle (left) or a technical nutrient cycle (right).

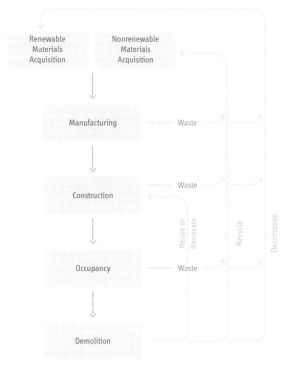

In the cradle-to-cradle life cycle of a product or building, all waste materials, including those resulting at the end of life, return to either biological or technical nutrient cycles, or are reincorporated into later steps in the life cycle.

doesn't refer literally to food that we throw out, but to all kinds of waste—organic, inorganic, industrial, residential—and signifies that everything we think of as garbage must become an input for another use. Landfills, by this measure, are wasted resources, a sign of gross inefficiency, and they represent a failure to follow the instructions in Fuller's *Operating Manual*.

McDonough and Braungart divide everything we might consider waste into two primary categories: biological nutrients and technical nutrients. Biological nutrients are materials that, after we are done with them, can be safely returned to the earth and become part of a new cycle. Technical nutrients are materials that do not easily break down when returned to the earth and therefore need to be kept in cycles of usage—they need to be recycled. Petroleum-based plastics are a good example.

There are also materials that are both unrecyclable and unsafe to put back into ecosystems (e.g., nuclear waste and toxic chemicals). Because these are so expensive to deal with and because they have no place in a cradle-to-cradle system, these are to be avoided at all costs. Composites of materials that cannot be separated after use and so cannot become either biological or technical nutrients are also problematic. McDonough and Braungart call these "monstrous hybrids."

The Triple Bottom Line

So far, we've been looking at green design in terms of environmental impacts. True sustainability, though, requires us to broaden our definitions to include aspects of *how* we live. How are the people who make things treated? How are their communities affected? How are the economic and social inequities among regions of the world dealt with? How do our buildings affect their occupants and local communities? This can be thought of as the fourth level of ecodesign, building upon the ecological foundations of the three Rs and the cradle-to-grave and cradle-to-cradle approaches.

In conventional business practice, the standard gauge of success is the bottom line: is the company making money? In the world of green business, an alternative

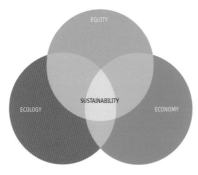

The overlap of ecology, economy, and equity is where we find sustainability.

The Nadukupam Vangala Women's Center (2008) was designed by Architecture for Humanity through hands-on design workshops with the community of Nadukupam.

gauge has evolved. The triple bottom line concept adds two criteria alongside the financial one: how the planet is treated and how people are treated.[5] The three bottom lines are frequently referred to as "people, planet, and profit" or "ecology, economy, and equity."

Putting numbers to ecology and equity is a very complicated and controversial process, but the concept that good business (and, as a corollary, good design) embraces these aspects of sustainability is not.[6] In practice, this concept can have several interpretations, ranging from not buying products made affordable only because they are produced by people who are not paid "living wages" to adopting social programs and design approaches like those of the Rural Studio, the Make It Right Foundation, or Architecture for Humanity, which promote "design for the other 90%."[7]

This also brings us back to the fundamental question of what sustainable design is and what its goals are. The classic definition of sustainable design actually derives from a United Nations committee's description of sustainable *development*.[8] Substituting "design" for "development" in their definition, we get "design that meets human needs while preserving the health of planetary life."[9] A balancing act, in other words. How do we provide for ourselves now without destroying the ecosystems that will enable future generations to survive?

What, then, does the goal of sustainability mean? Is it a useful term in communicating the intentions of eco-design? What *are* our goals?[10] The most basic of goals is to survive. Chances are that your primary survival needs—food, water, air, and sleep—are pretty well fulfilled. Once these are assured, the objective becomes providing the means to continue to survive. The conventional precepts of ecodesign involve setting the stage so that the things we need for survival are not in short- or long-term jeopardy. The loops are closed, and we take no more from the environment than can be returned or renewed.

But we need to question whether sustainability is truly our ultimate goal. If we define sustainability as the means to continue to exist, is that really a sufficient

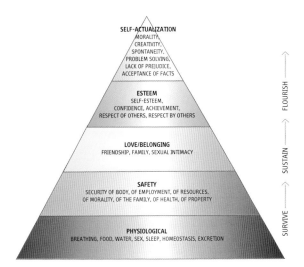

SELF-ACTUALIZATION
MORALITY,
CREATIVITY,
SPONTANEITY,
PROBLEM SOLVING,
LACK OF PREJUDICE,
ACCEPTANCE OF FACTS

ESTEEM
SELF-ESTEEM,
CONFIDENCE, ACHIEVEMENT,
RESPECT OF OTHERS, RESPECT BY OTHERS

LOVE/BELONGING
FRIENDSHIP, FAMILY, SEXUAL INTIMACY

SAFETY
SECURITY OF BODY, OF EMPLOYMENT, OF RESOURCES,
OF MORALITY, OF THE FAMILY, OF HEALTH, OF PROPERTY

PHYSIOLOGICAL
BREATHING, FOOD, WATER, SEX, SLEEP, HOMEOSTASIS, EXCRETION

FLOURISH
SUSTAIN
SURVIVE

Maslow's hierarchy of needs progresses from physiological needs to those that enable self-actualization. (Note: the scale "survive, sustain, flourish" to the right of the diagram was added by the author.)

aspiration? Many would argue that our reasons for existence, both as individuals and as a species, go beyond this to fulfillment in interpersonal or community or intellectual or spiritual senses. This state of fulfillment might best be termed flourishing and raises the accompanying question: how does design enable us not merely to sustain but to flourish?

If sustainability is not an adequate goal, what should we call this? What term could describe the attempt to go beyond "being less bad" and beyond "mere" sustainability to get to a point where design is not just minimizing negative effects but is encouraging positive impacts? There's been no consensus on this so far. One way to describe it might be "positive design," defined as the creation of an object or system that contributes to the fulfillment of real human needs while preserving or complementing the natural world.

This definition is not earth-shatteringly different from the one we started with, but it modifies two things. It refers to "real" human needs in order to differentiate needs from wants (flourishing would be a need; a larger television would be a want). In relation to architecture, this might mean addressing social and equity issues (such as the needs of low-income groups) or, on another level, analyzing the nature of the spaces we create, looking at what they add to or how they detract from our lives.

Regenerative Design

The second modification of our earlier definition of sustainable design adds "complementing the natural world," as opposed to simply maintaining it. The previous definition stated that the health of the planet should not be compromised but said nothing about repairing the damage that has already occurred.

This leads us to the ultimate level of ecodesign: taking care of all of our current and future needs as well as those of our planet (they are inseparable) *and* repairing those areas of our ecosystems that have been compromised or destroyed by human endeavors. This is no small goal in light of the demands we put on our ecosystems and the

The work planned for New York City's former landfill Fresh Kills, designed by James Corner Field Operations, is an example of regenerative design.

Another example of regenerative design, Vincent Callebaut's project
Anti-Smog (2007) includes many green aspects, such as a titanium dioxide coating that reacts with particulates in Paris's smoggy air to break
them down and dissipate the pollution.

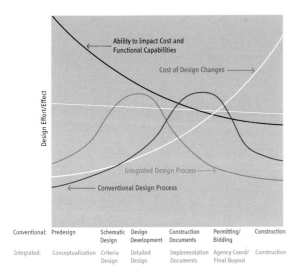

Conventional:	Predesign	Schematic Design	Design Development	Construction Documents	Permitting/ Bidding	Construction
Integrated:	Conceptualization	Criteria Design	Detailed Design	Implementation Documents	Agency Coord/ Final Buyout	Construction

A comparison of effort, effect, and cost over time in conventional design processes and integrated design processes (adapted from Construction Users Roundtable).

way we continue to view ourselves as separate and independent from the Earth. Examples of regenerative design (which is sometimes called restorative design), therefore, are hard to find. Some candidates include the reclamation of New York City's former landfill into a park with restored ecosystems and the dumping of retired (and stripped) subway cars offshore to help rebuild coral reefs.

The Cost Issue

We tend to look at the case for green design in terms of avoiding negative impacts. On the flip side, we can look at the positive impacts instead. The environmental gains are often obvious. Less apparent, though, may be the construction and operating cost benefits. The commonly accepted view is that green design and construction are more expensive, often prohibitively so. But more and more studies are showing that green buildings can cost the same as or even less than conventional ones, provided some fundamental green design concepts are applied.

In a conventional design process, the architectural work typically occurs first, followed by engineering and then construction. Often, however, this approach results in missed opportunities because of the lack of input from and coordination with all the parties involved in the project. Integrated design is the alternative process of including all primary contributors from the beginning, before design begins. Frequently a collaborative workshop called a charrette is held, and the entire project team—including consultants, owners, and contractors—meets to propose and discuss fundamental ideas. This has the dual purpose of making sure all parties are aware of what everyone is doing and, perhaps more significantly, encouraging brainstorming in which new solutions can arise.

For example, an architect's decision to specify triple-pane windows, which provide extra insulation but are more expensive than standard windows, will increase the construction cost. However, the specified windows will decrease the heating and cooling loads. If the mechanical engineer is involved in that decision, he or she may downsize the heating, ventilating, and air-conditioning (HVAC) systems, offsetting the cost of the windows.

The new high-efficiency windows may also result in *future* savings in the form of lower utility bills. In many budget decisions, though, only first costs are considered, a shortsighted approach that saves a few dollars up front while incurring much larger costs later on. Taking the long-term view, though, is especially difficult in cases when the building will be turned over to someone else after completion or when the occupant rather than the developer will be paying the utility bills. But even then, studies have shown that a building with lower operating costs will usually command a higher sale or rental price, justifying the initial costs.

Analyzing long-term costs involves looking at return on investment (ROI), sometimes referred to as the payback period. To give an overly simplified example, if installing a $20,000 solar panel leads to a savings of $2,000 per year in utility bills, the payback period is ten years. A real ROI calculation also takes into account inflation and interest rates and attempts to anticipate fluctuations in the cost of energy. Looking at the hard numbers of an ROI sometimes yields surprising results and tells us where to find the low-hanging fruit. For example, Kendall-Jackson, a winery in Northern California, has been undergoing a businesswide green conversion that examines all aspects of its operations, ranging from lighting to irrigation to

In these examples, the payback times range from well under a year to ten years (adapted from greenandsave.com).

Return on Investment (ROI) Table

	Payback Time in Years	Added Cost	Annual Savings	Ten-Year Savings	ROI
Programmable Thermostat	0.6	$115	$180	$1,800	156.5%
Windows	2.3	$70	$30	$300	42.9%
Graywater: Small Scale	5	$300	$60	$600	20%
Geothermal	10	$30,000	$3,000	$30,000	10%

pest control. The company found that many of its green programs resulted in very short-term payback periods. Upgrading their lighting to more efficient sources led to a 50 percent reduction in electrical usage and an ROI of less than a year. Installing a cool roof paid for itself as reduced air-conditioning demand in less than three years. Better controls on landscape irrigation, combined with planting native and drought-resistant species, yielded an ROI of just two years.

Further Benefits

There are other categories of ongoing potential savings that can more than justify the price of green design. For most businesses, the costs of labor far outweigh the costs of building and operating a facility, and design decisions that result in reduced labor costs can have quite a significant effect.[11] Many studies have shown that incorporating increased daylighting, improved artificial lighting, or better ventilation and air quality, to cite a few examples, increases productivity, decreases employee sick days, and lowers employee turnover. If the building is residential, making it healthier can create other benefits, both tangible and intangible, such as reduced medical costs and fewer days when children are home sick, keeping parents from work. We'll look further at this in "Indoor Environmental Quality."

Not to be left off the list of the advantages of green design are the positive effects it can have on its practitioners. It's tempting to see this new part of design as an added burden, requiring additional knowledge, coordination, time, and, if you've been practicing conventional architecture for a while, changes to the ways you work. The other side is that it can open up unexpected paths: new clients, fresh design influences, and increased personal satisfaction.

All told, the common perception that ecodesign is more expensive for clients and a burden for designers is more often than not incorrect. When ecodesign is incorporated well, we get a win-win situation in which everyone is better off. You don't have to be a tree hugger or an altruist to incorporate green design. Green design, as it has been suggested, should be just good design.[12]

The other misconception that we need to dispel is that ecodesign is a passing trend. Yes, we went through this once before in the 1970s. After that energy crisis abated, after the gas lines disappeared and oil prices fell back to "normal," the interest in energy conservation waned, too. Now, in the midst of what might be called the second generation of environmentalism, I think it's fair to say that it's not a fad this time. Very few people expect energy prices to remain low or to do anything but go up in the long term.[13] And on the regulatory side, more and more municipalities are requiring energy- and water-efficient design. Sometimes this is just for government-owned buildings, but increasingly, codes are being updated to incorporate environmental efficiency for all buildings. Ecodesign is becoming impossible to ignore; not only is it financially wise, but it may also be required.

Site Issues

Sitting over my desk is a Jenny Holzer piece that reads "Much was decided before you were born." There are many ways one can read that line, but what brings it to mind here is that it could be applied to architects and the topic of site design. Frequently, many site decisions—starting, of course, with the selection of the site—have been made before an architect is brought on board. This is not always the case, though, and when brought in sooner, the architect has the opportunity to affect these early and sometimes fundamental decisions.

Site issues tend to overlap with other aspects of design. Indeed, many ecodesign topics are interwoven with one another, which sometimes makes it difficult to assign them to specific categories or chapters. Site orientation, for example, has strong implications for passive-energy design, and will be reviewed in "Energy Efficiency: Passive Techniques." Light pollution, on the other hand, could be set in the energy and lighting section of "Energy Efficiency: Active Techniques" but is included at the end of this chapter as a site issue. Is daylighting a site-orientation or an active- or passive-energy topic? It certainly relates to both siting and solar angles, but it makes sense for our purposes to discuss it with artificial lighting.

Ideally, site selection should begin with considering some very primary issues. How will the building or development tie into the watershed? Will it have an impact on local biodiversity? Is there potential for locally produced renewable energy? Is there nearby supporting development and infrastructure, as in related businesses and public transportation? If this is a manufacturing facility, is there potential for collocation with complementary production, where, for instance, one business's waste can be utilized by another?

Sprawl and Development

As did a large percentage of the American population, I grew up in a suburb.[1] It seemed pretty idyllic at the time: a cul-de-sac where we played kick ball, plenty of lawn around the house, neighbors near but not "too near," no urban decay (this was the 1960s and 1970s), the mall "only"

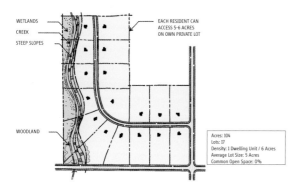

WETLANDS
CREEK
STEEP SLOPES

WOODLAND

EACH RESIDENT CAN
ACCESS 5-6 ACRES
ON OWN PRIVATE LOT

Acres: 104
Lots: 17
Density: 1 Dwelling Unit / 6 Acres
Average Lot Size: 5 Acres
Common Open Space: 0%

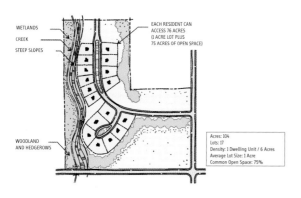

WETLANDS
CREEK
STEEP SLOPES

WOODLAND
AND HEDGEROWS

EACH RESIDENT CAN
ACCESS 76 ACRES
(1 ACRE LOT PLUS
75 ACRES OF OPEN SPACE)

Acres: 104
Lots: 17
Density: 1 Dwelling Unit / 6 Acres
Average Lot Size: 1 Acre
Common Open Space: 75%

A comparison of land use in a typical suburban development (top) and a cluster development.

thirty minutes away. On the other hand, the schools were not within walking distance, a quart of milk required a half-hour roundtrip drive, most of our working parents commuted by car into the city, and how I hated mowing that seemingly endless lawn.

That post–World War II suburban sprawl model was, arguably, a good and perhaps necessary thing in the 1950s. There was a huge need for inexpensive housing, and the new availability of cars and highways made the outward spread both possible and palatable. In short order, it became a national trend to leave the deteriorating urban core for the American dream of suburban home ownership. This trend, though, did not occur on its own. It was fueled by the construction of the Interstate Highway System, which made commuting by car feasible, and then by planning codes that promoted separation of land uses and minimum lot sizes for homes.[2] Though perhaps well intentioned, this set the stage for an increasingly fuel-dependent society.

Suburban sprawl is now being supplanted as policy by cluster development, smart growth, smart cities, and New Urbanism. Cluster development, in particular, has been around as a concept for several decades, but many zoning policies are still based on conventional planning. In a cluster project, rather than spacing the homes in a subdivision as far apart from each other as possible, the houses are closer and the remaining land is set aside for recreation or

Aerial views of a typical suburban development (left) and cluster development.

preservation. This has the added benefit of reducing development costs since, with homes closer together, roads and utility lines are shorter.

Cluster development doesn't really change the suburban model; it just makes it a bit more environmentally acceptable. It doesn't address the fundamental issues of transportation and ecofootprint.[3] Presuming energy prices continue to rise over time, the Levittown model upon which so much development has been based for the past fifty years will become increasingly unviable and undesirable. When gas is expensive, driving to get milk or commuting by car every day just does not make sense.

The benefits of walkable communities, where homes, offices, and retail and public spaces are located within walking distances, extend beyond saving gas (and money). They also include decreased air pollution and better health due to walking and biking instead of driving. Much of this argument has been codified by the Congress for the New Urbanism.[4] The most well-known New Urbanist development is probably Seaside, Florida. Unfortunately, it is an imperfect example in that it is a high-end resort community (as opposed to an economically diverse primary home and work community). But it does exhibit many of the goals of New Urbanism: homes, town centers, schools, stores, and parks that are within walking distance, and livable streets that are designed more for their community functions than for the flow of cars.

Arguably, the word *new* in New Urbanism is an inherent problem. Many critics have observed that the vibrancy and diversity of a city or town center cannot be created instantly, nor can it be fully conceived through planning. Cities and towns evolve, complete with wrong turns and unexpected junctures. Maybe time will enable New Urbanist developments to feel more organic and less sterile, but a frequent complaint is that they tend to look and feel like scenes from *The Truman Show* (which, in fact, was filmed at Seaside).

On the other hand, the forced urbanism of these towns is preferable to the alternative: the American landscape of sprawl, strip malls, and big-box chain stores. Whereas towns

The center of the New Urbanist town Orenco Station, Oregon.

organized on smart growth principles provide a base for further growth and evolution, the typical suburb, economically and physically segregated, does not have many ways to develop socially or become more ecological. Current economic pointers, actually, are indicating quite the opposite: suburbs are likely to become less desirable due to increasing transportation costs and inefficient, oversize homes.

What, then, is the future of suburbs? When we look at new planning visions, we also need to consider what to do with the many existing and sometimes outmoded structures we are left with: dead malls, subdivisions that have failed in the current economic crisis, and factories and office parks that are no longer viable. The suburbs are not without hope, and an enormous investment of resources has been made in these buildings and infrastructure, so it would be extremely wasteful to simply abandon or demolish them. A growing movement is looking at possibilities for their reuse.[5]

The same logic applies to renovation versus new construction. In ecological terms, the greenest choice is to use something that already exists, meaning an existing structure. (The next-greenest thing to do is to use land that has already been built on instead of untouched land.) Reuse and upgrading of existing structures is crucial for improving the efficiency of our overall building stock, as well. The number of new buildings is dwarfed by the quantity of existing buildings, and most of those are older, inefficient structures.[6] But by the year 2035, 75 percent of the U.S. building stock will be either new or renovated; and if those renovated buildings are more energy efficient than their current incarnations, that will make a sizable impact on total energy consumption.

This means we need a multipronged approach to development: an emphasis on building near public transportation and in urban areas with existing infrastructure; a focus on how to reuse the investment in buildings that are not in those areas; explorations of how to modify or reconceive existing suburbs so that they are less environmentally demanding (while not throwing away the economic and material investments already there); and an overall push to increase energy efficiency in both new and reused buildings.

Before (top) and after of Central City (2004), formerly known as Surrey Place Mall, in British Columbia, designed by Bing Thom Architects.

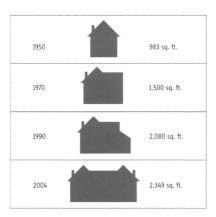

1950	983 sq. ft.
1970	1,500 sq. ft.
1990	2,080 sq. ft.
2004	2,349 sq. ft.

The average size of the American house has more than doubled in the last fifty years, while families themselves have become smaller (adapted from NAHB).

Size Matters

While in some ways the Levittown model has become the standard for the American landscape, that model has also evolved. Not only were the lots in postwar subdivisions often smaller, the houses themselves were more compact than today's engorged homes, which have come to be known as McMansions. Though American families are no larger than they were half a century ago (in fact, they are smaller), homes have increased in size about 250 percent. On the face of it, this might sound like a good thing, a sign of growth and success. But all that square footage has to be made of materials, has to be heated and cooled and lit, and has to be furnished and filled with belongings. That might be an acceptable trade-off if it actually made people happier, but it hasn't. Modern life has, instead, frequently become an unsatisfying game of keeping up with the Joneses; we continuously feel we want more when we see what our neighbors and friends have. It's a vicious cycle.

In *The Not So Big House: A Blueprint for the Way We Really Live*, Sarah Susanka makes a convincing case for smaller but better homes. Spend less, she advocates, on gratuitous spaces and features like double-height entry halls and formal living rooms, and put that money into details like storage areas, better materials, and more insulation. Both the client and the planet will end up better off.

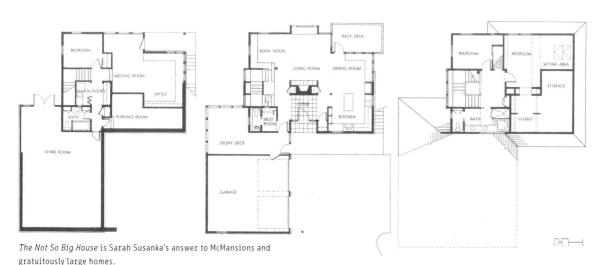

The Not So Big House is Sarah Susanka's answer to McMansions and gratuitously large homes.

Watershed

In cities and suburbs alike, buildings and pavement are spreading over increasing areas of land, leading to problems in managing stormwater runoff. In urban areas, stormwater is usually gathered in catch basins or storm drains along street curbs and then fed into a collection system. In less dense areas, there may be similar drains or open swales that lead to municipal systems or drainage retention ponds. In some old cities, such as New York and Chicago, the situation is further complicated by combined sewer systems in which the storm drains feed into the same pipes as sewage. When it rains, the sewage system is often overwhelmed, resulting in the discharge of raw sewage into waterways.

Our goal is to reduce, control, or store stormwater runoff, and there are a few ways to achieve this. One approach is to use permeable, or pervious, paving materials. These allow water to pass through them and seep into the ground, rather than accumulating and flowing above, and have the added benefit of providing some purification as the water channels through the rock and soil below the paved surface.

Another approach is to diminish the sudden impact of heavy rains by creating absorbent surfaces to take the place of nonabsorbent roofs. As you'll see in several sections of this book, nature has many models we can emulate or learn from.[7] For example, adding a growing medium and plants on roofs enables the building to act as a sponge. The water is still released, but it occurs gradually and much of it via transpiration—the plant equivalent of sweating—which also serves to cool the roof.

These vegetated roofs, known more popularly as green roofs, offer an advantageous symbiotic situation. They provide stormwater control, heat island remediation, building insulation, longer-lasting roofs, habitats for wildlife, and, depending on the type of green roof, the potential for gardening and other amenities.[8]

There are two types of green roofs. Extensive green roofs have shallow-rooted plants, usually sedums, in a shallow growing medium. Intensive green roofs can incorporate

Extensive green roofs (top) have shallow rooted plants and weigh less than intensive green roofs.

Impervious areas can be replaced with permeable materials and landscaping. This driveway has pervious pavers with grass growing in them.

deeper-rooted plants, sometimes even trees. The downsides to intensive roofs are that they are heavier and more expensive and they usually require irrigation. (Extensive roofs, if planted with native species, usually won't need irrigation after the first year or two.) In both cases, the plants and soil shield the roofing material from weather and ultraviolet radiation so that the durability of the roof is actually extended.

Green roofs are by no means a new concept. They are proven and popular in many parts of Europe, where they were originally adopted for insulation purposes and have a history dating back to the seventh-century Hanging Gardens of Babylon. A new interpretation of this idea is the living wall (also called a biowall or vegetated wall), which is similar in concept to a green roof but oriented vertically. The plants are usually attached to wire systems or set in planters that are gapped out from the facade.

Vegetated design is evolving from an add-on to an integral part of architecture. Designers such as Patrick Blanc are creating intricate sculptural walls. Other designers are developing vegetated surfaces that climb up and over buildings, sometimes even continuing indoors. At times they are merging organic with modern architecture, breaking down the old division between ecodesign and contemporary design, as well as the barrier between building and landscape.[9]

Intensive green roofs usually require irrigation and more maintenance than extensive green roofs (adapted from *Environmental Design & Construction*).

Characteristic	Intensive Green Roof	Extensive Green Roof
Soil	Requires minimum of one foot of soil depth	Requires one to five inches of soil depth
Vegetation	Accommodates large trees, shrubs, and well-maintained gardens	Capable of including many kinds of vegetative ground cover and grasses
Load	Adds 80 to 150 pounds per square foot of load to building structure	Adds 12 to 50 pounds per square foot depending on soil characteristics and type of substrate
Access	Regular access accommodated and encouraged	Usually not designed for public accessibility
Maintenance	Significant maintenance required	Annual maintenance walks should be performed until plants fill in
Drainage	Includes complex irrigation and drainage systems	Irrigation and drainage systems are simple

The realm of vegetated surfaces is expanding, as shown in this design for a Dallas project by Little Diversified Architectural Consulting.

Patrick Blanc, a botanist, developed the concept of the living wall and created sculpted layouts that can be thought of as vertical topiaries.

Urban or vertical farms, such as Living Tower by SOA Architects, attempt to address the carbon footprint of food transportation into cities.

A still newer concept is the vertical urban garden or farm: a multistory glass-enclosed structure that houses year-round agriculture to feed local residents, thereby reducing the carbon footprint inherent to transporting food into cities. Whether such farms could actually feed a city is still conjectural; regardless, the recombining of nature and farming with the city is a fascinating proposition.

Light Pollution

It wasn't until I was in my twenties, sitting on a beach distant from the suburban New York of my childhood, that I realized one could actually see the Milky Way. I was far enough from the city that the yellow-brown glow of reflected light—its light pollution—was beyond the horizon.

Programs to limit light pollution are often referred to as dark skies, and they are important for several reasons. Viscerally, the lack of connection to the stars represents another level of our separation from the natural world. Pragmatically, all of that upward-directed light is wasted energy—a more efficient design would direct the light only toward areas where it's needed. Additionally, light spillage, or light trespass, can be detrimental to humans and other species. It can interfere with animal life, disrupting nocturnal species and the migratory patterns of birds. Humans, too, have a daily cycle, circadian rhythm, which requires darkness at night. Since the invention of artificial lighting, we've been altering that cycle, and some studies indicate resulting health problems. Light trespass exacerbates this problem.

Fortunately, there are remedies available, some of which are already being adopted by local codes. Outdoor commercial lights, for instance, are now rated according to how much upward light they allow. And several cities have instituted regulations requiring that buildings turn off decorative lighting after a specific hour. A lit skyline can be beautiful, but it hardly needs to be fully illuminated at 2 AM; by limiting this excess, we also save energy.

The night sky in rural Texas.

Water
Efficiency

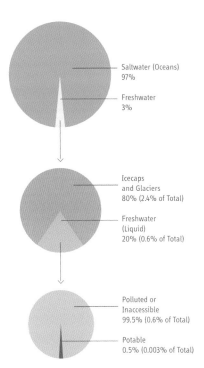

Saltwater (Oceans)
97%

Freshwater
3%

Icecaps
and Glaciers
80% (2.4% of Total)

Freshwater
(Liquid)
20% (0.6% of Total)

Polluted or
Inaccessible
99.5% (0.6% of Total)

Potable
0.5% (0.003% of Total)

Although approximately 70 percent of the Earth's surface is covered in water, only 0.003 percent is drinkable and accessible (adapted from USGS).

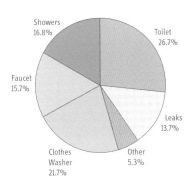

Showers
16.8%

Toilet
26.7%

Faucet
15.7%

Leaks
13.7%

Clothes
Washer
21.7%

Other
5.3%

More than a quarter of our indoor residential water use goes down the toilet (adapted from U.S. EPA).

In the previous chapter, we looked at water in terms of controlling storm runoff: that is, solutions dealing with an excess of water. The flip side of this issue is water conservation. While the Earth is a watery planet (about 70 percent of the Earth's surface area is covered by water), almost all of its water is either salty, frozen, or polluted, causing many experts to predict that our next big geopolitical conflicts, after oil, will involve water. Vast parts of the world do not have enough drinking water, and that includes major regions of the United States, as the recent droughts in the Southwest and Southeast have shown. Farther south, Mexico City has experienced its worst drought in fifty years and recently had to turn off the water supply over a holiday weekend. Water shortages lead to health issues, crop failures and famine, and even military conflicts as nations and regions make competing claims for rights to the water. Here in the United States, disputes between states are not uncommon.

Agriculture and power-plant cooling are the two largest consumers of water in the United States, but buildings consume 14 percent of our potable water.[1] And much of it goes down the toilet or onto lawns.

Landscaping

It can be argued that the great American lawn, ubiquitous across suburbs and office parks, is neither great nor American. Lawns are an idea originally imported from England, which means, among other things, that most grasses are not native to the land they are planted on, especially in arid climates. Lawns also tend to require fertilizers and pesticides, as well as dirty, noisy mowers and leaf blowers. One study, based on NASA satellite photos, concluded that grass is the most irrigated crop in the country.[2] The solution in most cases lies in minimizing lawn areas and using native species of ground cover and wildflowers instead of grass.

This needn't be viewed as a sacrifice; rather, it's an issue that requires questioning our assumptions. It's practically a given that buildings are surrounded by lawns. But why? Although it's nice to have an area to sit or play on, most lawns are merely decoration (and often not very

Before (left) and after of a lawn replaced with xeriscaping. Edible Estate Regional Prototype Garden #6 (2008) in Baltimore, Maryland (commissioned by Contemporary Museum Baltimore).

decorative at that). Natural growth is easier to maintain and ecologically preferable. In arid areas, it is embodied in a type of landscaping called xeriscaping (*xeros* is Greek for "dry"). The edible yards movement encourages another alternative: making the land productive by growing food in place of grass.

Gray Water

In addition to the techniques for controlling stormwater runoff previously discussed, rainwater can also be collected and stored for irrigation. Methods of harvesting rain range from do-it-yourself barrels to aboveground and belowground cisterns connected to roof drainage systems. Ironically, a few Western states actually prohibit rainwater collection on the basis that it restricts access to the water by those who are downstream.[3]

While harvested rainwater can sometimes be used for drinking and washing, it is generally limited to irrigation or indoor nondrinking uses and is included in the category of gray water, defined as water that is not clean enough for drinking purposes but not contaminated with waste.[4] (More heavily contaminated water, such as the water flowing out of the toilet, is called black water. Potable water is sometimes called white water.) A typical interior gray-water system captures drain water that does not contain organic waste, including water from showers, baths, bathroom sinks, and washing machines. With some filtration, this water can be

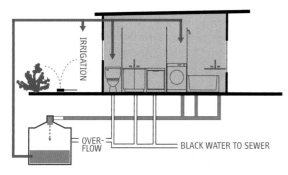

Diagram of a residential gray-water system.

used for irrigation. A more elaborate system utilizes gray water for flushing toilets. This requires not only separate drain lines for the gray-waste water, but also separate supply lines to bring the gray water to toilets. A roadblock here is that not all plumbing codes have been updated to allow gray-water installations.[5]

Water Efficiency

Gray-water systems reduce consumption by substituting slightly dirty water for fresh water. A more direct way to reduce consumption is to use efficient or low-flow fixtures and appliances. Some early low-flow fixtures (notably, toilets and showerheads) did not function well and became the source of derisive jokes, creating a legacy problem that deterred people from using them even after performance improved. The good news is that those problems have long since been overcome. Low-flow toilets today work at least as well as the older high-consumption models. By definition, a low-flow toilet uses less than 1.6 gallons per flush (gpf), compared to the 4 to 6 gpf by older models.[6] A newer standard for high-efficiency toilets (HETs) further reduces consumption to less than 1.28 gpf. HETs accomplish this either by limiting the flush volume or by utilizing a dual-flush system in which liquid waste is flushed with less water than solid waste, yielding an average of less than 1.28 gpf.

A more extreme option is the composting toilet, in which waste is diverted to a composting tank rather than to the sewage line. Little or no water is consumed, because water isn't used to transport the waste. Many people have trouble overcoming the ick factor, but composting toilets are useful where municipal sewage or septic systems are not available. Due to their water efficiency, they are also beginning to be employed even when conventional sewage options are available.

There are now several manufacturers of composting toilets and several variants of the systems involved. Some models use a tank placed directly under the toilet; others divert the waste to a composting tank in the basement, which may use heat to augment the composting process

The indoor component of the Eco-Machine at the Omega Center for Sustainable Living (2009), designed by BNIM Architects with John Todd Ecological Design.

The courtyard of the Sidwell Friends School (2006), designed by KieranTimberlake, is also a constructed wetland. Diagrams of the water system act as learning tools for the school's community.

(which, of course, requires electricity consumption). When maintained properly, they have no odor—in fact, they may smell less than conventional toilets, because the waste does not sit in the bowl—but they do require upkeep in the form of emptying the tanks from time to time. As with gray-water systems and waterless urinals, local building codes vary on whether composting toilets are permissible.

Urinals, too, can be waterless. The concept is that instead of being flushed with water, the waste is capped in the drain by a lighter-weight fluid that sits above it, preventing sewer vapors from escaping. The waste then runs down a conventional sewage line. The savings include water consumption and not having to install a water supply line and are offset to a degree by the need to replace the fluid periodically.

Toilets are a primary source of wasted water, but showerheads and kitchen and bathroom faucets can be reined in as well, often simply by changing the aerator at the tip of the faucet. Faucets that use sensors, however, are generally designed for purposes of hygiene (so you don't have to touch a potentially dirty faucet) rather than for conservation, and they may not actually cut down water usage. They also frequently require batteries to operate, creating both a maintenance and a waste problem, though some newer models use the flow of the water to generate power.

Many water-saving plumbing fixtures now carry a WaterSense label. Similar to the better-known Energy Star label, WaterSense is an efficiency rating, administered by the U.S. Environmental Protection Agency, covering toilets, bathroom faucets, and showerheads, as well as new homes in general.

Wastewater Treatment

Water efficiency deals with both intake (water consumed) and outflow (sewage). The standard methods of handling wastewater involve sending it to a municipal treatment system or, when none is available, a septic system. An environmentally better solution is on-site treatment using natural processes such as Eco-Machines and constructed wetlands.[7] Both are examples of biomimicry, the process

A drainage bioswale adjacent to a conventional street.

of studying how nature's systems work in order to devise our own. Eco-Machines, originally conceived by John Todd, involve processing sewage through a series of biosystems that break down the waste. Essentially, they amount to the infrastructural equivalent of a digestive system and are an integral part of envisioning buildings as whole and perhaps self-sufficient systems.

Depending on the type of waste being treated, as well as the site and local climate conditions, Eco-Machines may utilize indoor or outdoor components or both. Indoors, the system usually involves aerated tanks in greenhouselike environments, providing surface area for microbial organisms to break down waste and nutrients. These tanks harbor a healthy ecosystem of bacteria, plants, snails, and fish, which form the basis of the treatment process. Outdoors, constructed wetlands—basins that are lined to prevent leaching and planted to mimic some of the processes that occur in natural wetlands—have been used to treat runoff as well as sewage while simultaneously creating wildlife habitats. Bioswales are a simpler type of constructed wetland in which site runoff (not sewage) is directed through a drainage course that both guides and cleans the water.

While Eco-Machines and constructed wetlands differ somewhat in their methods (and are sometimes used together), they both attempt to produce buildings with a lower or even net-zero impact: buildings that are closer to self-sufficiency and less of a burden on the community and ecosystems around them. Taken a step further, beyond net-zero impact, natural wastewater treatment can become an example of regenerative design (discussed in "Ecodesign: What and Why"), offering additional benefits such as biofuels, fodder crops, fish, and ornamental flowers.

The term *net-zero* is usually applied to a building's energy consumption, but a larger view involves looking at all the systems and requirements of a building throughout its life. Since our planet has finite resources (the Spaceship Earth concept), it stands to reason that sustainable development has to avoid exhausting these resources.[8] In other words, it must have a net-zero impact.

Energy Efficiency: Passive Techniques

Energy efficiency is probably the topic that first comes to mind when discussing the ecodesign of buildings, and with good reason. The energy demands of the constructed environment are huge, and increasing the energy efficiency of buildings is perhaps the single most effective step we can take in reducing our environmental footprints.

Within energy efficiency, there are two general approaches: passive and active techniques. As you might expect, passive techniques consist of simpler, usually nonmechanical approaches, while active techniques tend to involve more advanced technology. As you might *not* expect, the passive/active distinction is not really about human involvement. Some passive approaches require active participation (such as opening and closing windows or vents), while certain active approaches (such as photovoltaic panels or automated lighting controls) may not need a human hand at all.

Another difference between passive and active energy efficiency is that most passive concepts are not new. Often they utilize tools or methods that are centuries old, ideas that have been in continuous use or that were left along the wayside when design in the Industrial Age seemed to make them unnecessary or superfluous. Many of these temporarily lost or forgotten techniques are now being rediscovered.

Since they are not new, most passive techniques are mature, time-tested concepts, not cutting-edge technologies in the way that active tools such as photovoltaics or light emitting diodes (LEDs) are. That means there are fewer unknowns and fewer things to go wrong. Passive tools also typically have fewer moving parts, so they require less repair or maintenance. Taken together, this makes passive energy efficiency simpler, more reliable, and usually less expensive than active energy efficiency. In fact, many ecodesigners believe that passive tools are the first steps to be taken because they tend to yield the most bang for the buck.

We can start understanding passive energy efficiency by looking to local design. Most types of indigenous architecture derived from necessity. In the days before

The north and south facades of the San Francisco Federal Building (2007), designed by Morphosis, have distinct designs in response to the differing solar conditions of the two sides.

heating and air-conditioning systems, for example, how were buildings cooled in the hot and humid Southeast? How were they heated during the New England winters? How did buildings take advantage of breezes in Iran or sun angles in New Mexico? That historic relationship between design and local conditions changed when the Industrial Age combined with modern architecture. No longer was building design at the mercy of nature. The same curtain-wall tower or wood-framed house could be inserted virtually anywhere in the world. And the design of each side of a building could be the same, regardless of the direction it faced. Not only could a suburban development house look exactly the same in different parts of the country, but it could also look exactly the same no matter its orientation. This made for a simpler, assembly-line style of building, suitable for the modern mass-market world, but it makes little sense in terms of responsive design. A south-facing facade, if energy consumption is at all a concern, needs to be different from a north-facing one. Similarly, a building facade at the latitude of Dallas, for instance, should be different from a building farther north in Buffalo.

Thermal Mass

The combination of latitude and seasonal changes in sun angle results in varying amounts of insolation—the amount of solar radiation received. Insolation is an important factor in active solar projects (as discussed in the following chapter), but it is also a critical component of passive solar design. The design for a passive solar building has to take into account the amount and angle of solar gain throughout the seasons and during the course of each day. When these are combined, building forms optimized in terms of footprint, massing, orientation, facade, and fenestration can be generated. To get there, it's necessary to break down the components of passive solar design. The U.S. Department of Energy (DOE) has a very simple outline explaining the five elements that collect and distribute solar radiation within a building, condensed here[1]:

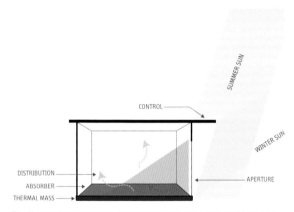

The five basic components of passive solar heating (adapted from DOE).

1. Aperture (collector): The large glass (window) area through which sunlight enters the building.
2. Absorber: The hard, darkened surface of the storage element.
3. Thermal mass: The materials that retain or store the heat produced by sunlight.
4. Distribution: The method by which solar heat circulates from the collection and storage points to different areas of the building. A strictly passive design will not use mechanical methods.
5. Control: Roof overhangs and other means that can be used to shade the aperture area during summer months.

In DOE terms, windows and other openings that admit light are apertures. Overhangs, awnings, and window treatments are called controls. The design of the controls will determine when and how much solar radiation is admitted into the building through the apertures. It is possible to look at each of these elements independently from an energy or a design perspective. That type of route is often taken when ecodesign is considered an added layer or afterthought rather than an integral starting point. As described earlier, that approach typically results in designs that are less innovative and fail to obtain the greatest environmental and economic advantages. It's the difference between merely adding overhangs to the windows on a south facade in order to reduce solar gain and envisioning the building as a system in which multiple elements are combined and coordinated.[2]

The objective of controls is to allow solar radiation into a building when it's needed (i.e., in the winter) and to minimize it when it's not (in the warmer months). Overhangs, when designed properly, can do that. Window blinds can too, but they require either user interaction or automated systems. Nature provides us with another method: deciduous trees can function as controls by virtue of having leaves in the summer and dropping the leaves in the winter. And they accomplish this with a negative carbon footprint. In colder climates, we can take further advantage of this ultimate organic shading product

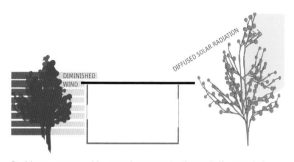

Deciduous trees provide natural summer shading and allow needed winter sunlight. Coniferous trees provide winter windbreaks.

by planting coniferous trees near the north facades of buildings, where they can cut down on cold winds in the winter while (depending on the latitude) providing high summer shading.

Once the controlled solar radiation is admitted into the building, it has to be managed, and that's where thermal mass comes into play. If left unmanaged, the heat from the radiation can cause the space to warm up rapidly, perhaps uncomfortably, and when the sun sets, the heat may be lost just as quickly. The solution is to create a building element that has the ability to absorb and retain solar gain so that the heating and cooling cycle of the day can be evened out. This involves two parts. First, a visible surface is needed to absorb the solar radiation. Appropriately, this surface is called an absorber. Since lighter colors reflect radiation and darker colors absorb it, a basic rule is that the absorber should be fairly dark in order to be effective. The absorbed radiation then has to be retained. This is handled by thermal mass: materials such as concrete, stone, or earth, which have the ability to store and then slowly reradiate the energy. A dark wood floor over concrete is a good pairing of absorber and thermal mass. The materials don't have to be separate, however. Dark-tinted concrete, for example, can serve as both.

The remaining element in the passive solar design diagram is distribution. In many passive systems, distribution is the gradual reradiation of stored heat from the thermal mass. But it can also be augmented by mechanical means, such as fans and blowers, or joined with passive ventilation systems.

Trombe walls can be thought of as a variation on the five passive solar elements described above. In a Trombe wall, the aperture becomes a larger area, and the absorber and thermal mass are placed parallel to the aperture with an air space between. The air trapped between the aperture and the thermal mass serves to insulate the mass so that it does not lose its heat to the outdoors. Instead, the heat moves through the thermal mass toward the interior. Depending on the density and thickness of the mass, it

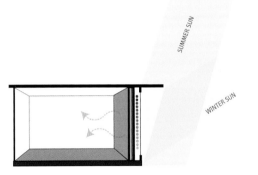

A Trombe wall can be thought of as a passive thermal mass turned vertically.

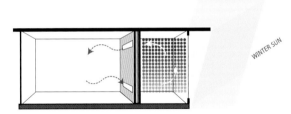

Trombe wall with operable vents and space for a sunroom.

arrives at the interior sooner or later. For example, if the mass is an eight-inch-thick concrete wall and heat travels through it at a rate of one inch per hour, then the heat will arrive indoors eight hours later—or approximately at sundown, when the outdoor air temperature starts to fall. By adding operable vents to a Trombe wall, even more control over heat dissipation can be gained. And by adding extra depth between the aperture and the mass, the space can become useful as a greenhouse or sunroom.

A Trombe wall can be thought of as combining a type of solar thermal collector with added insulation. In fact, there are versions of the concept in which the thermal mass takes the form of vertical tubes of water. Essentially, a Trombe wall creates an intermediate layer that buffers the internal space from the external climate while moderating temperature swings.

Double-Envelope Construction

The concept of a thermal buffer space can be extended to entire facades or even whole buildings, leading to designs that are basically buildings within buildings. Though this layering might appear to be a redundant and wasteful use of material, it can produce very efficient building envelopes when executed well. These double-envelope designs can be found in both low-tech wood-frame residential

Behind the facade of the Figge Art Museum (2005), designed by David Chipperfield, is an inner curtain wall; together they function as a double-envelope or double-skin system.

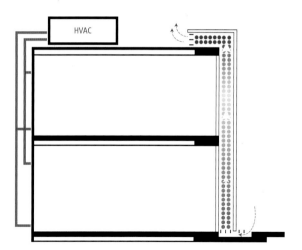

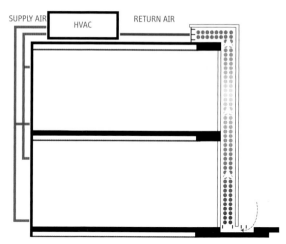

In the summer, hot air is vented at either the top of the building or the top of each floor, depending on the design. In the winter, warm air is directed to the heating system to preheat the colder outdoor intake air (adapted from LBNL).

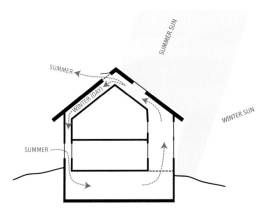

Diagram of an Enertia house's daytime airflows in winter and summer. The primary difference is the release of hot air through a vent at the peak during the summer. (Nighttime airflows not shown.)

construction and advanced curtain-wall buildings. In a simple form, a south-facing curtain wall has two skins and functions more or less like a Trombe wall but without the thermal mass absorber. Solar radiation causes air to heat up between the layers. The heated air is then either used to heat the building or vented out the top, depending on the season. Typically, a shading system is employed to control the amount of light and heat allowed into the building's inner skin. The outer skin may also double as a rainscreen protecting the inner layer.

When the concept is extended to wrap the entire building, it becomes a double envelope rather than just a double facade. An example of a double-envelope building is the Enertia house, a proprietary concept for a wood structure consisting of an inner primary space surrounded by a dynamic envelope in which airflow is adjusted with the season.[3] On a cold winter day, south-facing glazing warms up the air in the dynamic layer, which rises to the attic and releases its heat to the wood. The cooled air then circulates down the north face to the basement, where it is tempered by the thermal mass of the earth around it. At night, the circulation reverses as the exterior of the south face cools faster than the rest of the building. In summer, the attic's hot air is vented out the roof, which creates low pressure in the basement, where air is drawn in and cooled, again by the earth.

Earth Berming

Earth was mentioned previously as a type of thermal mass, and this leads to another approach to passive heating and cooling: embedding the building in the ground. Cave dwellings were, of course, the earliest example of this. Caves were inhabited undoubtedly because they were ready-made enclosures, but they also offered the advantage of natural temperature mediation by the surrounding rock and earth. Utilizing this form of insulation today does not necessitate a return-to-the-earth aesthetic, and it does not mean literally living in caves (though there are some beautiful cave homes found in places like Santorini, Greece). There are contemporary and architecturally interesting ways to update the

The semi-underground Becton Dickinson Campus Center (2008),
designed by RMJM, incorporates thermal mass and vegetated roofing.

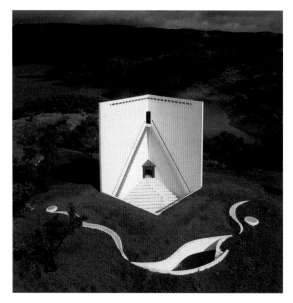

Exterior and interior views of Emilio Ambasz's House of Spiritual
Retreat (designed 1979; built 2004).

The proposed Monterey Bay Shores Ecoresort, designed by Bull Stockwell Allen, combines earth-bermed design with many other ecodesign principles, such as green roofs and regenerative use of brownfields.

N

GARAGE

BATHROOMS/
UTILITIES/
LAUNDRY

W — BEDROOM — BEDROOM — E

LIVING — KITCHEN — DINING

S

A diagram of a house layout that makes use of solar orientation.

cave, such as underground and earth-sheltered or earth-bermed buildings. Placing a building mostly or entirely underground is a highly efficient way to control temperature fluctuations; the problem, however, is in avoiding the aesthetic and emotional pitfalls of subterranean living. Emilio Ambasz's House of Spiritual Retreat demonstrates intriguing means of tackling this challenge without compromising access to natural daylight.

A less radical approach is to insulate part of the structure from heat loss either by building it partially underground or piling up earth against it. New England potato barns are a great example in which earth was packed along the two long sides of the building to keep the potatoes at a nearly constant temperature for winter storage. (Many of the surviving Long Island potato barns have since been turned into artists' residences and studios, presumably well insulated.)

When earth-bermed or partially buried buildings are combined with other ecodesign concepts, such as green roofs, the potential for integrating buildings into the landscape and minimizing their ecological and visual impacts increases. As with the discussion of vegetated design in "Site Issues," the line between artificial and natural begins to blur.

Solar Orientation

For a building to effectively use thermal mass for solar gain or for insulation, it has to be oriented advantageously. In practice, this means that the best orientation for a building is with its major axis running east-west, so that it can have passive solar apertures facing south and offer an insulated barrier with fewer openings to the north. In a residential example, the most efficient layout would locate frequently used daytime spaces to the south and more utilitarian or night-occupied spaces, such as bedrooms, to the north.

South-facing windows, of course, are also subject to summer heat gain (as are east- and west-facing windows) unless they are shaded, as described earlier. North-facing windows, especially at high latitudes, should be smaller or high quality (or both) to minimize both heat loss and infiltration by cold northern winds.

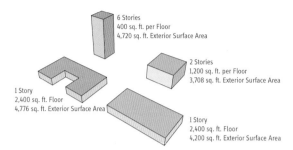

6 Stories
400 sq. ft. per Floor
4,720 sq. ft. Exterior Surface Area

2 Stories
1,200 sq. ft. per Floor
3,708 sq. ft. Exterior Surface Area

1 Story
2,400 sq. ft. Floor
4,776 sq. ft. Exterior Surface Area

1 Story
2,400 sq. ft. Floor
4,200 sq. ft. Exterior Surface Area

In general, building envelopes with less exterior surface area relative to volume are more efficient than irregularly shaped single-story buildings and very tall buildings.

Solar orientation is not the only factor. Prevailing winds and natural or artificial obstructions figure into the equation as well. For instance, a cliff (or a high-rise building) to the south may undermine all your otherwise valid planning.

Surface-to-Volume Ratio

A factor as fundamental as a building's overall mass and shape can be significant as well. Since heat loss and heat gain occur through the building's envelope, it follows that a building that has less exterior exposure will be more efficient. This means that multistory buildings—to a point—are more efficient than single-floor structures (assuming similar types of construction). This is one of the reasons why people living in cities have lower ecofootprints than rural and suburban denizens. In general, the goal is to have a low surface-to-volume ratio, that is, as little exposed surface relative to the amount of interior space as possible. This is a bit at odds with some other design goals, especially daylighting. A large floor plate, for instance, may be more efficient for heating and cooling, but it means deeper, darker spaces farther removed from daylight, views, and natural ventilation. Trade-offs like this, in which conflicting goals are weighed and balanced, are not unusual in ecodesign. In some cases, tools like energy modeling and life cycle analysis can guide decisions, but simulations and analyses are always incomplete and their necessary objectivity can be a shortcoming. For instance, an energy model can't take into account the emotional benefits of daylighting. Subjectivity also comes into play when considering the relative significance of ecological impacts, as we'll discuss in "Labels and Ratings: Measuring Ecodesign." Therefore, we cannot rely exclusively on formulas for solutions. Rather, it's important to take the information gleaned from models and studies and, in a sometimes intuitive process, attempt to arrive at innovative solutions that transcend the pure data.

Windows and Glazing

Creating a large southern exposure doesn't mean that an elevation should have as many windows as possible. There's a point of diminishing returns, determined by the size of the windows, their thermal qualities, the thermal qualities of the floor or walls that the sunlight falls on, and, of course, the climate patterns. A building in a hot region with a low-thermal-mass floor would not be a good candidate for a large expanse of south-facing windows (unless it incorporated effective daylight controls). On the other hand, a building sited farther north with a stone floor and insulating windows might make great use of southern windows (provided that these windows are well engineered).

Window terminology has become a lot more involved than it used to be. In the 1960s, architects had a basic choice between single-pane and insulated, or thermal-pane, glass. In all but the most comfortable climates, insulated glass is now the minimum standard. The advanced choices include triple-pane, thermal-break, gas-filled, low-emissivity, and other options. To simplify decision making, Energy Star and the National Fenestration Research Council have devised a label that lists five qualities:

1. U-factor is the inverse of the better-known R-value. It is a measure of a window's ability to prevent heat from escaping. A lower U-factor means less heat will escape. The ratings generally fall between 0.20 and 1.20.

2. Solar heat gain coefficient (SHGC) is a measure of the window's ability to block incoming heat from sunlight. SHGC numbers are between 0 and 1, with a lower number indicating less heat transmission. In most cases, a lower number is therefore better.

3. Visible transmittance is an indicator of how much light comes through the glass. Like SHGC, it has ratings between 0 and 1, with 1 indicating greater transmittance.

4. Air leakage is an indicator of how much air passes by infiltration relative to the size of the window. It is expressed in cubic feet per minute per square foot of window (cfm/sq. ft.) As you might expect, less infiltration is better.

5. Condensation resistance is how well the window resists the formation of condensation on the interior surface. Ratings are between 0 and 100, with a higher number indicating better resistance.

World's Best Window Co.	
Millennium 2000+	
Vinyl-Clad Wood Frame	
Double Glazing • Argon Fill • Low E	
Product Type: **Vertical Slider**	

ENERGY PERFORMANCE RATINGS

U-Factor (U.S./I-P)	Solar Heat Gain Coefficient
0.35	**0.32**

ADDITIONAL PERFORMANCE RATINGS

Visible Transmittance	Air Leakage (U.S./I-P)
0.51	**0.2**

Condensation Resistance	
51	**—**

Manufacturer stipulates that these ratings conform to applicable NFRC procedures for determining whole product performance. NFRC ratings are determined for a fixed set of environmental conditions and a specific product size. NFRC does not recommend any product and does not warrant the suitability of any product for any specific use. Consult manufacturer's literature for other product performance information. www.nfrc.org

The National Fenestration Rating Council's window label.

Low-emissivity (low-e) coated glass has become a highly popular product. Low-e coatings reflect infrared light while allowing visible light to pass through, lowering the SHGC and leaving visible transmittance unchanged.

More recently, gas-filled windows have become widely available. The gas, usually argon or krypton, replaces air between the panes of insulated glass. This gas reduces the convective movement of heat between the panes, increasing the window's thermal efficiency (though not at high altitudes). Higher-efficiency windows combine low-e with triple-pane and insulating gases and then further extend the technology to make "super windows" with heat mirror films and added spacers, resulting in windows that can almost provide the equivalent R-value of a wall. As with the discussion of facade orientation and design, the optimal properties of windows facing different directions may vary.

The frame of a window also contributes significantly to its environmental values, and opinions vary on which type of construction is ecologically preferable for low-rise structures.[4] By many gauges, vinyl windows are the best performers and are usually the least expensive; however, vinyl is a contentious material in the eco world. Wood frames have the disadvantages of durability and maintenance, and they may be constructed from endangered species. Aluminum and vinyl cladding, applied over wood, are attempts to balance out these issues. Fiberglass, like vinyl, raises some ecological concerns about its manufacture and disposal, but its embodied energy is lower.[5] Aluminum frames have poor thermal resistance and high embodied energy (unless made from recycled sources). So, as with many ecological choices, the answer is complicated by trade-offs and depends on the unique circumstances of the project.

In ecodesign, an answer is almost never one-size-fits-all. Rather, answers are derived from context and are full of counterpoints and geo-specifics, such as where the window is made, how long it will last, the size of the budget (for construction and for operations), and what the building's heating and cooling sources are.

Insulation

Those yellow or pink fluffy strips of insulation, stuffed between studs and rafters, have become a ubiquitous symbol of increasing energy efficiency. Indeed, from a thermal barrier point of view, a frame wall without insulation is hardly better than no wall at all. Standard fiberglass insulation, however, has some significant drawbacks. It typically contains formaldehyde, and its fibers can be irritating or even dangerous, as anyone who has installed this type of insulation can attest. Furthermore, it is not good at filling gaps, particularly those around pipes and wiring. Although versions of it have improved (a few no longer contain formaldehyde and some are made with recycled content), the issues with the fibers themselves and the difficulty of achieving a quality thermal barrier remain.

There are alternatives to fiberglass. A predecessor is mineral wool, a manmade fiber made from either minerals (called rock wool) or from blast-furnace slag (called slag wool). It is generally thought to be safer than fiberglass but is more expensive. A newer substitute is made from cotton or recycled denim. Its great advantage is that you don't have to wear a hazmat-type suit to install it, and since it is made from plants (unlike fiberglass), it is biodegradable. The disadvantage is cost—it can be anywhere from 50 to 100 percent more expensive than conventional fiberglass (an increase that may or may not be made up for in reduced labor costs).

These types of insulation come in rolls, called batts, but there are other forms available. Blown-in insulation, also known as loose fill, is useful for retrofitting existing walls and attics, among other situations. The typical procedure for adding insulation to a wall is either to remove the top of the exterior cladding or drill holes in the interior sheetrock in order to access the gaps between framing members and then blow the loose fill in through these openings. Until recently, fiberglass was the prevalent form of loose fill. Now cellulose, usually made from recycled newsprint, has become more common. Like cotton batts, cellulose is treated with nontoxic fire retardants and does not contain formaldehyde. Early versions of this material

Common Types of Insulation	R/inch
Fiberglass Batt	3.1–4.30
Rock Wool Batt	3.1–4.00
Cotton Batt	3.1–3.70
Cellulose Blown	3.7
Open-Cell Foam	3.6–3.8
Closed-Cell Foam	5.8–6.8

Comparison of R-values for some popular types of insulation.

had a tendency to settle within the walls, resulting in less insulation at the top, but newer formulations and blowing techniques have minimized this problem.

A significant advantage of loose fill over batt insulation is that it is better at filling gaps and less-accessible areas, such as those around intersections, electrical boxes, and pipes. Foamed-in-place insulation is even better at this. The installation involves spraying the foam, which then expands, filling gaps in the process. There are two basic types of spray-foam insulations: open-cell and closed-cell. Open-cell foams expand much more than closed-cell, growing to as much as one hundred times their initial volume and yielding R-values of close to four per inch. Closed-cell expands comparatively less but is denser and creates a higher R-value per inch, as much as twice the open-cell R-value. For this reason, open-cell installations require thicker cavities. They must also be protected within enclosed walls, because the dried foam is softer than closed-cell.

Spray foams no longer deplete the ozone layer and are increasingly made from biobased formulations rather than the predominant petroleum-based material. However, installers must wear protection due to short-term toxicity, and the EPA is currently investigating potential post-occupancy issues. The other downside is cost; spray foams tend to be more expensive than fiberglass batts.

Cool Roofs

With thermal mass, the objective is to gather and absorb heat. On roofs, though, the goal is reversed. For a few reasons, especially in the summer, heat should be reflected away. One is to minimize heat gain inside the building. The typical dark-colored roof, whether asphalt shingle or a bituminous flat roof, is a great absorber—useful in our thermal mass diagram, but not at the top of a building, where heat tends to accumulate. Another reason to reflect heat away is to address a phenomenon known as the heat island effect. Typically, built-up areas are several degrees warmer than surrounding less dense neighborhoods. In large part, this is due to the percentage of surface area, especially of pavement and roofs, that is covered in dark materials. Making roofs in light colors reflects much of that solar radiation and helps to alleviate both interior and exterior heat buildup.

There are several ratings systems for roofing materials. The most common gauge is albedo. It rates the degree of reflectivity of a material, running from zero (for total absorption) to one (for total reflectivity). Energy Star–rated buildings with flat roofs must use roofing with an albedo of at least 0.65; those with sloped roofs require material with an albedo of at least 0.25.

A material's albedo may not fully describe its heat-absorbing properties. A metal roof, for instance, may be highly reflective but also have low emissivity, causing it to heat up more than a nonmetal material with the same albedo. The solar reflectance index (SRI) is a newer gauge that rates both reflectivity and emissivity.[6] A standard black surface has an SRI of zero and a standard white surface has an SRI of one hundred. The LEED heat island effect credit requires an SRI of at least seventy-eight for low-slope roofs and twenty-nine for steep roofs.

The downside of a cool roof is the loss of heat gain in the winter. Ideally, we'd have roofs that would change color throughout the year, and, in fact, these are in development. This type of material research exemplifies the combination of new technology with time-tested concepts.

Radiant Barriers

Another method of reducing summer heat gain from roofs is to install a radiant barrier. This is a reflective surface—placed below the roofing and rafters or at the attic floor—that reduces the amount of solar heat that penetrates the attic or upper story of the building. It can also help contain heat loss in the winter. For a radiant barrier to work, it needs to have an air space of at least 3/4 inch adjacent to the reflective side of the barrier (which can face in or out).

It's debatable whether it makes sense to use a radiant barrier in conjunction with a cool roof, since the cool roof will already reflect much of the solar heat gain. It can't hurt and will still assist with winter heat loss, but the cost may not be justified by the savings in air-conditioning.

Cooling effect of a radiant barrier.

Radiant barriers do not help reduce the heat island effect; they are primarily for reducing internal heat gain and the resulting air-conditioning loads and generally affect only the upper story of a building. So in a high-rise structure, the reduction of cooling will be less significant relative to the overall load. Similarly, the reduction in heat gain resulting from a cool roof (as with a green or vegetated roof) is felt only at the top of the building, whereas the reduction of the heat island effect is tied more to the ratio of roofed area to open space and is unrelated to the height of the building.

Ventilation and Circulation

To this point, we've looked primarily at building envelopes in terms of how to store heat or keep it in or out. That would be fine if our sole intention were to control the inside temperature and the building were in a climate where the outdoor temperature were not comfortable. Except perhaps for an arctic research lab, this is usually not the case. In most locations, there are times of the year or day when the outside air is pleasant and it makes sense, if for no other reason than to save energy, to ventilate a building with that air rather than with mechanically conditioned air. Beyond that, there are periods when we can utilize natural ventilation in place of mechanical cooling, even when the outside air is less than ideal. It requires, though, relearning some older, perhaps forgotten, techniques, as well as a better understanding of alternative natural systems.

The first rule of air movement (at least for this discussion) is that hot air rises.[7] Over the ages, building designs have made use of this fact to enable air circulation, typically by creating chimneys or tall spaces in which rising hot air generates a draft, pulling air from the lower parts of the building. The process is referred to as a stack or chimney effect. This explains why open-front fireplaces actually make buildings colder: the movement of air up the chimney requires that outside air be drawn into the room to replace it. The hot air from the fire is sent up and out the chimney, while cold outdoor air is brought into the room. The only place that is warmer, aside from the chimney, is the area directly in front of the fireplace.

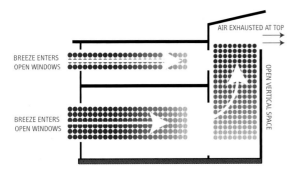

Illustration of natural ventilation combining prevailing wind with the chimney effect.

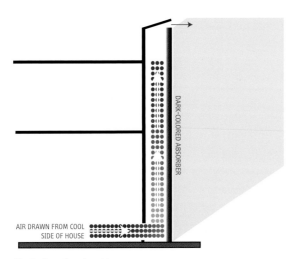

Illustration of a solar chimney.

Solar chimneys at the Sidwell Friends School. Note the extensive green roof surrounding the chimneys.

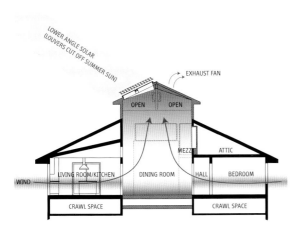

Proposed addition of a solar atrium to an existing courtyard-style house, designed by David Bergman Architect (black structure is existing; gray is proposed).

This counterproductive cooling can be put to intentional use in warmer weather to naturally cool and ventilate spaces using what's often called a solar chimney. The effect can be achieved by creating a tall space vented at the top, so that as the air warms, it can flow up and out. It can be augmented by using sunlight to heat up the chimney and the air inside it so that it rises faster. A chimney like this would have a southern exposure and, for the greatest impact, a dark surface to absorb solar radiation.

At the Sidwell Friends School (2006), in Washington, DC, designed by KieranTimberlake, solar chimneys serve several of the classrooms. The chimneys have south-facing glass so that their interiors function like greenhouses. To make the chimneys a learning experience (an example of didactic "visible green," discussed in "The Future of Sustainable Design"), the architects placed telltales and wind chimes at the inlets to the chimneys.

The chimney effect doesn't require a literal chimney or tower. For a recent renovation, my firm proposed adding a skylit atrium to the center of a house and opening the surrounding rooms to it so that prevailing winds could circulate air from the outside in. Then, as the air became warmer under the skylight, it would exit through vents at the top of the atrium. In combination with exhaust fans, the chimney effect could be expected to dramatically reduce the need for air-conditioning.

Traditional Persian wind catchers are another inventive example of ventilation chimneys. In the hot, dry environment of present-day Iran, the wind catchers have openings on all sides, so the wind can blow into one side of the chimney, creating positive pressure that circulates air down into the building. Then as the interior air heats up, it rises out the leeward, negative-pressured side of the wind catcher. The added twist is that the buildings also have ground level intakes that siphon air along underground water reservoirs called *qanats*. The air is cooled and moistened by the qanat and then admitted into the building, where it mixes with the air brought in by the wind catcher. Working together, this system is able to keep spaces cool during the hot Iranian summer day.

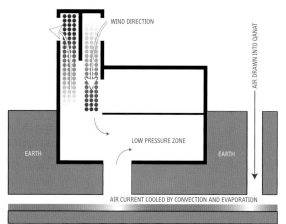

Photo and illustration of a Persian wind catcher and qanat (adapted from worldarab.net).

In the illustration: WIND DIRECTION · AIR DRAWN INTO QANAT · LOW PRESSURE ZONE · EARTH · EARTH · AIR CURRENT COOLED BY CONVECTION AND EVAPORATION

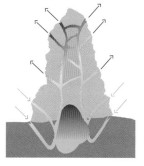

Photo and illustration of a termite mound, demonstrating how passageways and vents control the temperature.

As ingenious as this system is, it's humbling to realize that humans aren't the only creatures to employ such a method. In parts of Africa, there are structures that, if scaled to human size, would be the equivalent of hundreds of stories tall. These are remarkable for several reasons. First, they require no structural members and no engineering. Second, they require no HVAC systems in spite of the fact that they exist in an environment that can range from 35°F at night to 104°F during the day. And third, they are built by termites.

Termite mounds are made of clay mixed with termite saliva, which hardens into a material that can last long after the colony has died and, in an example of the wasteless systems of nature, becomes a nutrient for plants. But the more extraordinary aspect of the mounds, from the point of view of ventilation, is how the interior of the mound, despite the extreme daily swing of outdoor temperature, is maintained within a half a degree of 87°F without the aid of compressors, boilers, ducts, or fans. The mounds have hundreds of openings built into them, which are opened and closed by the termites to regulate the airflow. The openings lead to shafts running throughout the mound and sometimes hundreds of feet below it. The termites bring moist soil up from the lower levels to humidify the interior as needed.

Understanding termite mounds and putting this knowledge to use—as several buildings have—is a great example of biomimicry. In Harare, Zimbabwe, the team of Mick Pearce and Arup designed a commercial building that imitates the termite mound system with numerous inlets throughout the building and an array of ventilation chimneys on the roof. Combining these with other passive solar techniques (a central atrium, limited glazing, shaded northern windows—this is in the southern hemisphere—and thick masonry construction for thermal mass), the building is able to operate without any air-conditioning system at all and is comfortable on all but a handful of days each year.

A variant of this concept has also been utilized for a corporate headquarters designed by Kohn Pedersen Fox in Madrid. As in the Persian wind catcher designs, air is

Council House 2 (2006) in Melbourne, Australia, designed by Mick Pearce, employs a ventilation system derived from the termite mound concept.

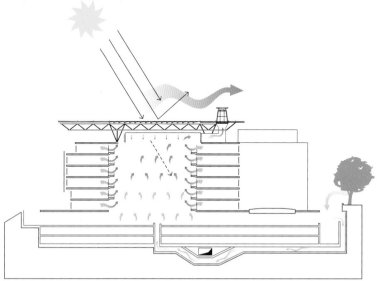

The Endesa Headquarters (2002) in Madrid, designed by Kohn Pedersen
Fox, uses an interior atrium, which the designers describe as "the
lung of the building," fed by air cooled in an underground passage and
vented through chimneys.

brought in from the ground level and cooled in a tunnel below the parking levels. The cooled air is then circulated through a central atrium and, as it heats and rises, is vented out the roof.

Many of these ventilation concepts work well in dry environments (Madrid gets quite hot but not humid) but aren't as applicable in humid climates. Dehumidification is a more difficult though not unsolvable problem in terms of energy efficiency. The solutions, however, usually involve mechanical systems, and that places them in the next chapter, "Energy Efficiency: Active Techniques."

Active approaches also tend to focus on efficient sources of energy, whereas passive techniques emphasize designing buildings to consume less energy from inception. The cheapest form of energy is energy not consumed. Environmentalist Amory Lovins calls this avoided consumption "negawatts."

The Breezeway House (2009) in Utah, designed by Brach Design Architecture, is a certified Passive House.

Passive House

Perhaps the most advanced application of this approach to energy efficiency is the Passive House movement. With roots in Germany, where it is called *Passivhaus*, it is beginning to take hold in the United States as well. The fundamental idea is a building that is superinsulated with very tightly controlled ventilation and air filtration. It embraces commonsense ideas concerning solar orientation and thermodynamics, combined with efficient massing that keeps the surface-to-volume ratio as low as possible. Adherents of this technique argue that it is more practical to cut the energy demand in the first place than to look for alternative ways to generate it. Their studies show that the long-term costs of a Passive House building (despite the name, Passive House principles may apply to commercial and large buildings, not just homes) are far less than a conventional structure or one that employs other ecodesign approaches and that the increased cost of construction, which can be minimal, is more than recouped in energy savings over time. Buildings can obtain Passive House certification by fulfilling specific requirements, which we'll discuss in "Labels and Ratings: Measuring Ecodesign."

Energy Efficiency: Active Techniques

Passive energy efficiency is usually grounded in basic concepts of thermodynamics: rates of energy flow through materials, the movement of heat through air. As a result, passive approaches usually involve low-level technologies that are relatively uncomplicated and have few moving parts, and they are often the first line of attack in the quest for energy efficiency. Superefficient or Passive House designs, which push passive energy efficiency to its limits, may decrease or even eliminate heating and cooling loads. But passive techniques alone will not achieve the goal of net-zero energy or carbon-neutral buildings, particularly when the energy demands of modern conveniences like appliances and electronics are included. No matter how efficient buildings and technology become, they will always draw some amount of energy. Accommodating these energy drains, therefore, involves looking at both how to make buildings and equipment run more efficiently and how to generate energy from alternative sources. This chapter will examine methods of reducing a building's energy requirements through active technologies while meeting the remaining energy needs through local, renewable power generation.

The objective is not necessarily to create completely self-sufficient buildings. Off-the-grid buildings are useful in remote areas, where the environmental and economic costs of bringing in power or fuel may be prohibitively high, but in developed areas, maximum efficiency may be more advantageous than self-sufficiency. Is on-site renewable power environmentally preferable to, say, a remote wind farm or tidal power? This is another example of an ecodesign question that does not lend itself to a single answer. In this case, the answer depends on the availability of on-site renewable energy (how much wind or insolation or geothermal potential is present), the types of off-site power sources available and their transmission distance from the building, the power intensity of the building, the ability to store energy, and myriad other factors. The bottom line is that we must design buildings that require as little energy as possible and then provide that energy in the most environmentally benign way possible.

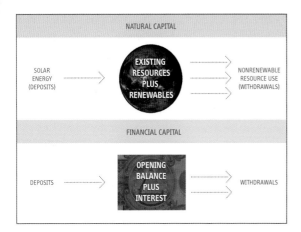

NATURAL CAPITAL

SOLAR ENERGY (DEPOSITS) → EXISTING RESOURCES PLUS RENEWABLES → NONRENEWABLE RESOURCE USE (WITHDRAWALS)

FINANCIAL CAPITAL

DEPOSITS → OPENING BALANCE PLUS INTEREST → WITHDRAWALS

One way to think about our use of the planet's resources (natural capital) is to compare it to a bank account. We can make withdrawals from the account only if they are less than the deposits (solar income from the sun) and interest (renewal of materials).

The concept of living off "current solar income" dictates that the only resource we can use without replenishment is energy from the sun. This is among the most fundamental rules of sustainability. If we do not live off current solar income and choose instead to expend our nonrenewable assets, we will run out of one or more of them sooner or later.

The next two sections examine the most direct, active methods of using solar energy: solar thermal collectors and photovoltaic panels.

Solar Thermal Collectors

Many of the technologies presented in this chapter are relatively new; some are cutting-edge. Solar thermal collectors, however, are an older and fairly mature technology. Rudimentary systems have been around for more than a century. A greenhouse is a type of solar collector (in much the same way that the interior of a car sitting in the summer sun is).

Modern solar collectors circulate fluid through a series of heat-absorbent tubes, often covered with glass panels (small-scale Trombe walls, essentially). The fluid is heated by the incoming, absorbed sunlight and used either directly or indirectly for hot water or space heating. In an open system, the fluid is regular water and it is used directly, perhaps for plumbing or, more commonly, for heating a pool. The potential problem here is that the water in the system has to be clean enough for consumption. Additives such

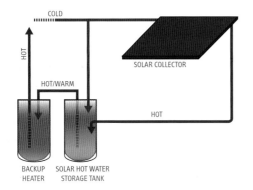

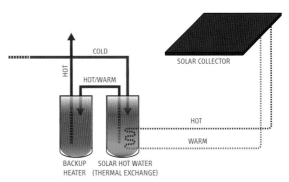

Illustrations of open and closed-loop solar thermal hot-water systems (adapted from southface.org and homepower.com).

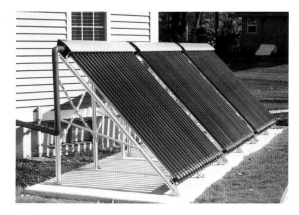

Solar thermal panels may have exposed collection tubes like this or may have the tubes behind a clear covering.

as antifreeze cannot be included, which means the fluid is subject to freezing. For that reason, most solar collectors use a closed indirect system in which solar-heated fluid (containing an antifreeze) is then piped through a transfer tank where it gives up its heat to the circulating water in the plumbing or heating system.

Since solar collectors are a time-tested technology, their advantages and drawbacks are relatively well known, as are their costs and benefits. Depending on the application, local utility rates, and availability of government incentives, the payback period for solar collectors is generally between five and twenty years. They are not the most aesthetically pleasing energy-efficient technology, unless they are visually integrated into the design, but they are among the least risky. To improve their effectiveness, they can be used in combination with water-efficient plumbing, such as low-flow showerheads and faucets that minimize demand for hot water, or passive solar techniques that reduce the need for heat.

Photovoltaics

Some photovoltaic (PV) panels may look similar to solar collectors because both often are installed as angled arrays of glass-covered rectangles on rooftops or in fields, but they are fundamentally different. Solar collectors use radiant heat from the sun to heat a fluid directly, while PV panels employ a more complicated process to convert solar radiation to electricity. Unlike solar collectors, PV technology is still evolving, with technical advances and new methods improving efficiency and feasibility, as well as creating potential new applications.

A conventional PV panel, which resembles a solar collector, uses a crystalline-silicon cell to convert light to electricity. Explaining how this works is beyond the scope of this book, but the U.S. Department of Energy's Energy Efficiency and Renewable Energy website provides an excellent description of the physics involved.[1] PV panels generally cannot feed directly into a building's electrical system, because the panels' output is direct current (DC), not the alternating current (AC) utilized by most of our

Conventional PV panels are mounted on top of buildings or nearby.

systems, appliances, lighting, and electronics, requiring a converter or transformer. (Ironically, most electronic devices and some lighting reconvert the power to low-voltage DC. Unfortunately, this results in a loss of efficiency.)

But what about when the sun goes down or it's cloudy outside? There are two solutions. The first is to use batteries to store power generated during the day. If the system generates enough electricity to both power the building during the day and store power for the night, then the building can be off the grid, meaning it does not need to be attached to an outside power source. The downside is that batteries, which an off-the-grid building requires to store energy, are cumbersome, expensive, and toxic when not disposed of properly.

In many cases, it is more practical to forgo energy independence in favor of generating PV power when the sun is available and then drawing from the power company when it is not. This isn't necessarily a drawback. In fact, PV systems can complement grid systems. For example, when the sun is out and the PV system is able to generate more power than the building needs, excess power is sent to the utility company. The electric meter runs backward, indicating that the utility company is drawing (and paying for) excess power generated by the system. This is called "net metering"; many utility companies now permit this practice even though the grid wasn't initially set up for it. One of the goals of the smart grid is to further enable onsite distributed energy, as opposed to remote, centralized power generation. With net metering in place, a PV system makes money during the day and spends it at night.

This concept has advantages beyond your utility bill. Peak power demand occurs on hot, sunny weekdays when air-conditioning systems strain the grid and sometimes result in brownouts or rolling blackouts. These circumstances are, happily, when PV panels perform at their best. Grid-tied PV systems augment the power network when it needs it most while drawing from the grid during off-peak periods, when there is excess capacity and power is cheaper. This essentially flattens daily power demand and allows the grid to operate much more efficiently.

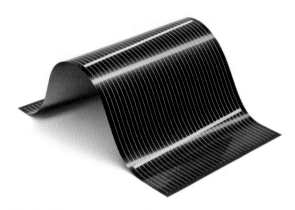

Thin-film PV is next-generation technology and opens many design possibilities with its thinness, flexibility, and potential translucency.

Thin-film PV applied to roofing shingles, an example of BIPV.

Another BIPV example, in a project by SRG Partnership.

The technology for conventional crystalline-silicon PV panels has progressed, but these systems are often seen as ugly appendages tacked onto buildings. Many well-intentioned homeowners have been stymied by architectural review boards or homeowner associations that consider PV installations eyesores. A newer type of PV offers the potential to overcome this and other issues of conventional panels. Known as thin-film panels or amorphous silicon panels, these new PVs are thinner than the familiar rooftop add-ons.

Thin-film PVs can be manufactured simply and inexpensively. Some production techniques are similar to ink-jet printing; the output from a thin-film-PV machine resembles a roll of metallic paper. Beyond cost savings, this technology is exciting because it opens up design possibilities for incorporating PVs into building materials, making them a part of the building rather than an appendage. This new way of utilizing PVs is called building-integrated photovoltaics (BIPV). Examples include thin-film panels applied to roofing shingles, which are then installed in place of or alongside conventional shingles. Thin-film has also been applied to standing-seam metal roofing and incorporated into spandrel and vision glass.

One remaining issue with respect to PVs is how much electricity a building can expect to generate and whether it will actually be cost-efficient. The calculations, which involve roof area and slope, latitude, weather patterns, site shading, etc., can get pretty complex, but simplified calculators are available online.[2] Incentives, which vary by state and municipality, can also affect cost feasibility. The Database of State Incentives for Renewables and Efficiency is a good source for checking utility, local, state, and federal incentives and tax benefits for both renewable energy and energy efficiency.[3]

Wind Energy

Expansive wind farms—with wide-blade turbines fanning out over hilltops or oceans—have become icons of the renewable energy movement. To some people they are majestic; to others they are noisy, ugly bird killers.

The potential exists to incorporate wind turbines into building design, such as this mixed-use tower by Oppenheim Architecture + Design, so that they become an aesthetic element, perhaps even driving the design concept.

Vertical axis turbines are not as dependent on wind direction and offer more aesthetic options than conventional turbines.

The same disparate opinions can be found regarding distributed wind power—smaller wind turbines mounted on or alongside buildings. There is some controversy as to whether small-scale wind turbines are in fact cost-effective. In concept, generating power locally rather than at distant wind farms or other power stations makes a lot of sense. *Environmental Building News*, however, concluded in 2010 that "it's actually pretty hard to get wind turbines to perform well on buildings and, even if you can, the economics are not very good."[4]

Wind turbine technology, though, is bound to improve, and its costs are likely to come down as new, better-looking, quieter, and more efficient turbines are developed. Just as PV is progressing into BIPV, the design of turbines is evolving from appendages that look like afterthoughts into sources of building-integrated wind. They can be large and very visible, as in a design statement like the Bahrain World Trade Center, or smaller and more discreet.

Wind turbines can also vary in shape, from conventional spinning propeller blades to vertical axis turbines, which rotate like corkscrews. The latter geometry allows the turbines to operate independently of wind direction, occupy less space, and generally have a more interesting aesthetic. As with PV panels, it's crucial to check local site and weather conditions and look for economic incentives to determine whether wind power is feasible for a project.

Mechanical Systems

Even superinsulated passive solar buildings usually require supplemental mechanical heating and cooling in most regions of the world. And with these buildings especially, controlled mechanical ventilation is needed in order to inject fresh air into their tight envelopes. Providing thermal comfort and maintaining indoor air quality beyond what can be achieved by passive systems are, in most types of buildings, handled by HVAC systems.

Heating and cooling are among a building's most energy-intensive functions. One way to diminish the energy needed is to *move* heat rather than create it. Instead of

The Greenway Self-Park (2010) in Chicago, designed by HOK, is one of the more visually interesting attempts to synthesize local wind generation and building design.

producing heat with a furnace, heat pumps move ambient energy from one location to another. This is accomplished by evaporating liquids or condensing gases. The evaporative and condensing processes absorb or release energy in the form of heat. The gas or liquid is then circulated into the building, where the process is reversed.

Air-source heat pumps draw energy from or release energy into the air outside, often using a split system with indoor and outdoor coils. For small projects, such as residential additions, a mini split system uses pipes that connect an outdoor compressor to an indoor wall- or ceiling-mounted blower unit that directly heats or cools a room without the use of air ducts. There are several disadvantages to ducts. They may take up valuable space or require that ceilings be lowered to conceal them. From an energy point of view, ducts lose efficiency over distance, primarily through joints and turns in the ductwork.

Because outdoor air temperature varies, air-source heat pumps, especially in colder climates, may not be a sufficient source of energy for heating and cooling a building. Fortunately, a more stable source is available: the ground. The concept of using earth to moderate a building's thermal mass was previously discussed in terms of earth berming and underground construction. Similarly, ground-source heat pumps (GSHPs), sometimes referred to as geothermal or geoexchange systems, take advantage of

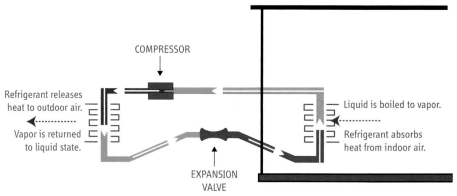

COMPRESSOR

Refrigerant releases heat to outdoor air.

Vapor is returned to liquid state.

Liquid is boiled to vapor.

Refrigerant absorbs heat from indoor air.

EXPANSION VALVE

Diagram of the cooling cycle of an air-source heat pump. The heating cycle works in reverse (adapted from DOE/EERE).

the relatively constant temperature below ground to heat or cool spaces (depending on latitude, the temperature at six feet below the surface will remain steady at somewhere between 45°F and 58°F).[5] To tap the subsurface temperature, pipes are typically laid underground, and a liquid circulating through the pipes is either heated or cooled by the ground before being pumped into an exchange tank where its heat (or coolth) is transferred to the HVAC system.

The most common GSHP systems are horizontal or vertical closed-loop systems. When the amount of available land area relative to the volume of space to be heated is large, the pipes are generally laid horizontally in shallow trenches. In more dense developments, where there is not enough land area to accommodate a horizontal layout, the pipes are installed vertically, like wells.

There are many advantages to using GSHPs. They require substantially less electricity than conventional heating systems; they provide good humidity control; and because so much of the system is below ground, they take up less usable space. They also have fewer moving parts compared to other systems, making them very durable. What's more, unlike air-source heat pumps or conventional air-conditioning systems, they do not create outdoor noise. The primary disadvantage is up-front cost; it may take a considerable amount of time to recoup it through diminished utility bills.

Once these sources of heating and cooling are established, a system for distributing the energy is needed. Conventional air-distribution systems have several drawbacks. One of them is that indoor air temperature can become stratified, as cool air settles at lower levels and hot air accumulates at ceilings. This is actually the opposite of what we ideally want, especially in heating seasons. In the winter, hot air is wasted when it rises above head level, and it is more likely to be lost through the ceiling, particularly if the ceiling is not insulated or is located directly under the roof. Additionally, this warm-above-cold stratification is not a good method to heat people. In terms of both comfort and productivity, it is preferable to have warm feet and cooler, more alert heads.[6]

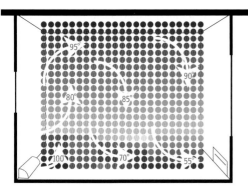

Conventional heating systems usually result in stratified, uneven heating and drafts (adapted from buildinggreen.com).

Radiant floor heating evenly distributes heat along the floor and results in a gentle stratification, concentrating heat where it's most needed (adapted from buildinggreen.com).

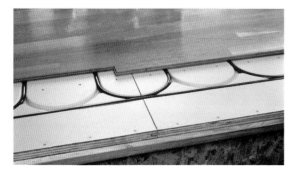

In addition to laying tubes within a concrete slab, radiant floor systems can consist of tubes laid in pre-routed channels between layers of wood.

This can be achieved through a radiant heating system. In a hydronic radiant floor system (there are also electric versions), heated water circulates through tubes laid below the finished floor. The heat is transmitted directly to occupants via radiation, which, as opposed to convection, does not utilize air as a medium. This is how the sun—the ultimate radiant system—heats the Earth from above and through the vacuum of space. Radiant heating results in less air movement (moving air feels cooler, which is helpful in summer but not in winter) and reduces dust and allergen levels. Though it's counterintuitive because hot air rises, radiant heating can also be installed at the ceiling.

Radiant systems can be used for cooling as well. The challenge when employing radiant cooling is in not allowing the indoor air temperature to fall below the dew point, which causes condensation unless the air is dehumidified. An increasingly popular method of radiant cooling is by chilled beam. In this approach, chilled water is circulated through beamlike ceiling structures. It utilizes both radiant cooling and convection: as the room's air warms, it rises to the ceiling, where it is cooled by the chilled water lines. The cooled air then circulates down the space.

As mentioned earlier, peak electrical loads occur on hot weekdays in summer, resulting in spikes in demand on the power grid. Grid-tied PV systems can help alleviate this demand. Thermal energy storage can also help even out the cycle of demand. This strategy uses inexpensive off-peak power to make ice or to chill water at night and then cool the building during the day using that stored thermal energy.

Another cooling technique to consider—one so straightforward that it almost counts as a passive energy technique—is wind chill. Simply running a ceiling fan can reduce the effective temperature by 4°F to 5°F and substantially cut the cooling load of a space. According to the Florida Solar Energy Center, raising the thermostat of an air-conditioning system by two degrees can result in a 14 percent savings in cooling-related energy use.[7]

A key to controlling HVAC demand (alongside the energy-efficient systems described earlier) is to design a tight building envelope. Concepts such as Passive House favor the idea of minimizing or even eliminating the need for mechanically produced heating and cooling. However, the inherent problem of tight buildings is their lack of fresh air. The challenge is to devise a way to bring fresh air in without compromising the energy efficiency of an otherwise well-insulated building. (The "Indoor Environmental Quality" chapter looks further at the need for air circulation.) Conventional construction allows—and sometimes relies on—air infiltration through windows, doorways, and other passageways. The problem is that this provides fresh air by default, as opposed to providing it when, where, and how we want it.

What's needed is a system that exhausts the stale air without losing its thermal conditioning (heating, cooling, humidifying, or dehumidifying) while pulling in fresh air. That outside air, however, is unconditioned, and injecting it into the space forces the HVAC system to work harder. The solution is to use an air exchanger: either a heat recovery ventilator (HRV) or an energy recovery ventilator (ERV). These ventilators contain heat exchangers that transfer the expelled air's desirable properties to the incoming fresh air without mixing the two air streams. Stale air is displaced by fresh air without throwing away the energy already expended to heat or cool it. An ERV takes this one step further, transferring moisture as well as heat, which is important for cooling cycles.

STALE HUMID COLD AIR TO OUTSIDE

FRESH WARM DRY AIR FROM HOUSE

FRESH COLD DRY AIR FROM OUTSIDE

STALE HUMID HOT AIR FROM HOUSE

Diagram of an HRV in heating mode. The circulation reverses for cooling (adapted from iaqsource.com).

HRVs and ERVs can be incorporated into a building or house in a number of ways: they can be independent systems, tied into bathroom and kitchen exhausts, or integrated into the HVAC system. The relative advantages of HRVs compared to ERVs are debated.[8] ERVs are more expensive, but in some regions they further cut down air-conditioning and dehumidification loads.

Hot-Water Efficiency

Domestic hot-water systems (for heating tap water, as opposed to hot-water space heating) are another significant consumer of energy in buildings. Typically, especially in homes, water is heated in a gas-fired or electric tank so that it is available as needed. The problem is that the tank has to keep the water hot at all times, regardless of usage. Newer tanks with better insulation lose less heat but still suffer the need to heat water that is not being used.

An alternative method is to use on-demand heating (also called tankless hot water). Though on-demand units have been in use elsewhere for many years, they are only now becoming popular in the United States. When hot water is needed, the unit turns on and instantly heats the water, thus eliminating the energy wasted in maintaining the temperature of stored hot water. On-demand units are made in sizes for a single bathroom, multiple rooms, or an entire house. Their relative efficiency, compared to conventional hot-water tanks, depends on several factors, including the size and type of plumbing layout and the level and frequency of demand.

Another significant benefit of the on-demand unit is that, because it is much more compact than conventional hot-water tanks, it can be located in a small recess in the wall or in a cabinet. Many models have freeze protection, so they can be installed outdoors. Perhaps the greatest benefit, though, assuming the size of the unit has been correctly specified, is that you'll never run out of hot water midshower again.

Electric on-demand units, it should be noted, require a sizable electrical service, because it takes a lot of power to heat the water that fast. Frequently, that means that gas

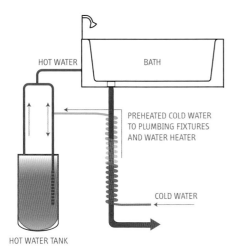

HOT WATER

BATH

PREHEATED COLD WATER
TO PLUMBING FIXTURES
AND WATER HEATER

COLD WATER

HOT WATER TANK

DWHR systems recover the wasted heat from hot water sent down the drain.

units are preferred, but the trade-off is that gas units need to be exhausted directly to the outside (unless the unit itself is outdoors).

Even with an efficient hot-water system, much of the hot water literally goes down the drain. A very simple method has been devised to recover some of the lost energy: a drain water heat recovery (DWHR) system, which basically consists of copper tubing wrapped around the drainpipes of bathtubs and showers. The water supply to the hot-water system (with or without the use of a tank) is routed through the copper coils and is warmed by the outgoing shower water. The coils don't fully heat the water; rather, they raise the temperature enough so that the water heater doesn't have to work as hard.

Efficient Lighting

Not since the advent of the environmental movement's three Rs has a single action gained as much popular significance as the use of compact fluorescent lamps (CFLs).[9] While CFLs are not the game-changing environmental saviors that some claim, they are a useful, albeit interim, technology. What makes them important is how efficiently they produce light. Incandescent light is a more familiar source of secondary light, and to many it is more pleasing, second only to sunlight. But incandescent lights employ a technology that has remained essentially unchanged since Thomas Edison's design of the late nineteenth century. It works fundamentally the same way as a toaster: a metal filament is electrically heated until it glows. Incandescent bulbs convert less than 10 percent of incoming electricity into light; the rest is emitted as heat. The primary difference between an incandescent bulb and a toaster is that the toaster is slightly more efficient at generating heat.

Lightbulb efficiency—the technical expression is "lamp efficacy"—is measured in terms of how much electricity is needed to produce a certain quantity of light, or lumens per watt (LPW). Keep in mind that electrical usage is measured in watts, not volts. We've grown accustomed to thinking of the relative intensity of a light source in terms of wattage, but this is actually only an indication

The filaments of a toaster and an incandescent bulb work in exactly the same way, which explains the wasted heat emitted by the bulb.

of how much energy a lamp is using, not how much light it is creating. Different light sources have varying efficacies, meaning they use different amounts of wattage to produce equivalent levels of brightness. For example, a 26-watt CFL produces approximately the same amount of light as a 100-watt incandescent lightbulb. This means that a CFL is around four times more efficient (or efficacious) as an incandescent bulb.

Incandescent lightbulbs have an efficacy of 10 to 20 LPW (typically in the low end of that range), which is consistent with the fact that they waste more than 90 percent of the electricity they consume. Halogen lamps, which are basically pressurized incandescent lightbulbs, have slightly higher efficacy, with LPWs in the upper end of the same range. CFLs improve on those numbers considerably, jumping up to 50 to 60 LPW. (This explains why a 26-watt CFL can have the same brightness as a 100-watt incandescent lightbulb.) Tubular, or linear, fluorescent lamps have slightly better efficacy than CFLs, ranging from 60 to 90 LPW depending on their size and age. Older and thicker T12 tubes are less efficient than the newer, slimmer T8 and T5 sizes.

Other types of light sources are available as well, notably high-intensity discharge lamps. Some of these have very good efficacy ratings, but they come with baggage. For one, certain types—like those garish yellow streetlights—have poor color rendition. Another problem is their slow strike time, meaning they take awhile to turn on and reach full brightness. Strike time can also be a minor issue with fluorescents. They may take a minute or so to reach full output, but they turn on instantly at a usable intensity. Metal halides take much longer to warm up, which makes them good for use in streetlights or in stores and warehouses, where they remain on for an extended period of time, but not for applications with intermittent usage.

Another advantage of CFLs is that they are long lasting. A typical incandescent lamp will last anywhere from 750 to 2,000 hours, whereas most CFLs are rated to last at least 8,000 hours. That means we can't compare

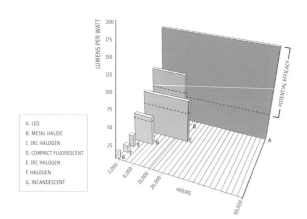

A. LED
B. METAL HALIDE
C. IRC HALOGEN
D. COMPACT FLUORESCENT
E. IRC HALOGEN
F. HALOGEN
G. INCANDESCENT

This chart shows two characteristics of our primary light sources: efficacy and bulb life.

This ad for GTE in 1970 is probably referring to its standard cold white fluorescents. The facing page was a sepia-toned version that said "not any longer," implying that warm white fluorescents had solved the light-quality issue of fluorescent lighting.

a single incandescent lamp to a single CFL. It's necessary to compare the costs and electrical consumption of approximately eight incandescent lightbulbs to one CFL. Suddenly, paying four dollars for a CFL doesn't seem so bad, and that's without counting the time saved in replacing bulbs less frequently.

CFLs and fluorescents, however, have suffered from a legacy problem. Early versions were less than pleasing. They buzzed, flickered, and rendered skin pallid. Early fluorescents, equipped with magnetically driven ballasts, could even cause seizures. But today's fluorescents have electronic ballasts that, in addition to being more energy efficient, neither buzz nor visibly flicker. Color rendition has become dramatically better as well. Warm white fluorescents were an early improvement, but they weren't enough to convince most of the public. More recently, fluorescents and CFLs with color temperatures matching those of incandescent lightbulbs have been introduced.

Color Temperature

Color temperature is not an intuitive concept. People generally prefer warm light, and one would think this refers to warmer temperatures, but it's actually the opposite. There are a few ways to visualize the concept of color temperature. The midday sky is blue when temperatures are hottest, while at twilight the sky is composed of reds and oranges, "warmer" colors that appear during the coolest part of the day. Likewise, the hottest part of a flame is the blue portion, not the red.

Color temperatures are measured in degrees Kelvin (K), which is calculated as degrees Celsius (C) plus 273. Therefore 0°C equals 273°K. In terms of visible light, the temperature of midday sunlight is approximately 6000°K, that of an incandescent lightbulb is between 2700°K and 3300°K, and a candle burns at approximately 1850°K. The interesting thing to note is that even though they are far warmer-looking than daylight, we tend to dislike cool white fluorescent lamps, which have a color temperature of around 4000°K, and we generally prefer incandescent-level temperatures at or below 3000°K. The

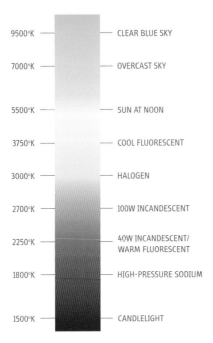

9500°K	CLEAR BLUE SKY
7000°K	OVERCAST SKY
5500°K	SUN AT NOON
3750°K	COOL FLUORESCENT
3000°K	HALOGEN
2700°K	100W INCANDESCENT
2250°K	40W INCANDESCENT/ WARM FLUORESCENT
1800°K	HIGH-PRESSURE SODIUM
1500°K	CANDLELIGHT

Color temperature is measured in degrees Kelvin, and "warmer" colors actually indicate lower temperatures.

actual temperature of daylight, when emitted from lamps, appears much too cold for most uses.

But that's not the whole picture. Color temperature tells us what the light coming out of the lamp looks like, but it does not provide a sense of how objects will look when seen under the light. For that, we need a gauge called color rendering index (CRI), which ranges from 0 to 100, with 100 being the highest rating, theoretically rendering colors the most accurately. Both incandescent lightbulbs and the sun have a CRI of 100. Early fluorescent lamps were pretty bad, with CRIs in the 60s. Newer models range from the mid to upper 80s, a range that, to most people, renders color nearly as well as incandescent light.[10]

Fluorescents, CFLs, and Mercury

There is, however, one small but critical issue with fluorescent lamps. They all require a minuscule amount of mercury, approximately four milligrams per lamp. Mercury is toxic, even in low concentrations, to humans and most other species. The problem is twofold: what happens when a used lamp is disposed of, and what happens if one breaks in a living area or work site? Burned-out lamps should not be put in general garbage; they should be recycled through appropriate facilities. Homeowners can check their municipalities or bring them to certain retail stores. Businesses usually need to use lamp collection services. For the disposal of broken lamps, the EPA has simple but important guidelines for cleanup and ventilation.[11] (You *don't* need to call in professionals with hazmat suits.)

Fluorescents would be a good energy-efficient solution if not for the mercury, which is why they are only an interim solution. To put the mercury issue in perspective, it's important to weigh the use of mercury in fluorescents against another, much larger source of mercury pollution: the burning of coal to produce electricity. In the United States, approximately 50 percent of our electricity is produced by burning coal. Residue from this process, called fly ash, contains mercury. Most of this fly ash is sent to landfills or storage facilities where it can eventually escape into the air and water. So as long as a significant portion of electricity production is coal-based—meaning, for the foreseeable future—power usage contributes to mercury pollution. According to the EPA, the electricity needed to illuminate an incandescent light for five years results in the production of ten milligrams of mercury. Compare that to a CFL, which requires one quarter of the energy, generating only 2.4 milligrams of mercury for five years of use; CFLs are obviously preferable in this respect. This assumes, however, that the mercury in the lamp does not escape into the environment, which might happen when a lamp breaks or is tossed into a landfill. Even in that worst-case scenario, the total mercury emitted is around 6.4 milligrams, which is still significantly less than the mercury output resulting from the electricity needed to power the fixture with incandescent bulbs.

CFLs have yet to overtake incandescent lightbulbs as the standard household light fixture, in part because of consumer reluctance or lack of familiarity, but also because buying a CFL can be more complicated than buying an incandescent. You need to check socket type, color temperature, and the shape (twisty or bent tube). In an effort to simplify this, Energy Star established a new type of socket, different from the conventional screw-base socket. It's a twist-lock design, designated GU24, that all new "dedicated CFL fixtures" will use. Because the sockets of these lightbulbs are not interchangeable with those of incandescents, an energy-efficient light fixture cannot, either by accident or intentionally, be fitted with an incandescent lightbulb.

GU24-base CFLs come in two varieties: one-piece integral ballast models, which look like the kind currently used to replace incandescents, and two-piece versions in which the ballast is separable from the lamp. The lamp portion of a CFL will last around eight thousand hours, but the electronics—the ballast—will probably last much longer, perhaps forty thousand hours. With a two-piece CFL, you can keep using that ballast after the lamp burns out. (Linear, or tubular, fluorescents are not made with integral ballasts; they have separate ballasts located either in or near the light fixture.) Despite these advances, there is still a strong stigma associated with fluorescent lighting, and

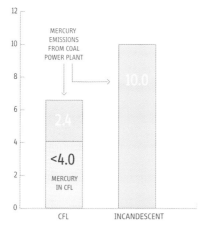

The mercury emitted from burning the coal needed to run an incandescent bulb is still greater than that from the worst-case scenario of a CFL, in which the lamp's mercury escapes into the environment (adapted from U.S. EPA).

It is indeed possible to design residential space using fluorescent lighting. This loft, designed by David Bergman Architect, uses incandescents on only a portion of the living room track. Tubular fluorescents were used to provide general as well as some decorative lighting, and recessed lights throughout are CFLs.

this will be hard to overcome unless we call it something other than fluorescent or are able to show how friendly fluorescent lighting has become.[12]

Another aspect of the stigma concerns dimming. Early dimmers for incandescent lights were primarily an amenity used to control the amount of light and create ambience, and they did not save energy. As the technology evolved to solid-state, dimmers gained the ability to conserve energy as well. (See "Lighting Controls" later in this chapter.) When used with incandescent lamps, dimmers will both cut energy consumption and extend the life of the lamp. But fluorescent lamps cannot be dimmed as simply as incandescents can; in fact, some fluorescents cannot be dimmed at all.

With the introduction of electronic ballasts, it has become a bit easier to dim fluorescent lamps, but it's still not a simple task. They often require expensive ballasts with coordinated dimmers, though some CFLs have integrated dimming ballasts designed to work with standard dimmers. In either case, dimming CFLs does not produce the romantic low-level glow to be had from incandescents. Fluorescent manufacturers generally claim that they dim to 5 or 10 percent, but that's misleading. Visually they appear to dim to perhaps 50 percent of full intensity. Then, depending on the equipment, they either shut off or flicker if you try to dim them further. Dimming, therefore, is another reason to label fluorescent lighting an interim solution.

Light Emitting Diodes

Fortunately, a solution to both the mercury problem and the dimming concern is rapidly taking over the lighting industry: light emitting diodes (LEDs). These are to incandescent lamps what solid-state circuitry is to the vacuum tubes in old radios. In fact, LEDs are frequently referred to as solid-state lighting. They have several advantages over incandescent and fluorescent lightbulbs. They are extremely energy efficient, or, to be more accurate, they are currently as efficient as fluorescents and have the potential to become far more efficient in the future, with anticipated efficacies reaching up to 200 LPW. This is an astonishing number compared to today's 10 to 20 LPW for incandescents and 50 to 60 LPW for CFLs. LEDs also last far longer than other light sources.

Measuring the longevity of an LED is a bit problematic, however. When a manufacturer says that its incandescent lamp lasts one thousand hours (or that its CFL lasts eight thousand hours), it actually means that half the lamps tested will no longer continue to work after this many hours. It's the average time before burnout. LEDs do not burn out the same way. They gradually lose intensity over time, fading rather than suddenly burning out. At what point, then, should the LED be considered burned out, or no longer intense enough to be usable? To answer this issue, the industry adopted a standard cutoff of 70 percent; that is, once an LED lamp has faded to 70 percent of full intensity, it is considered burned out. Most manufacturers claim that this occurs after approximately fifty thousand hours. That's roughly six times the life span of a CFL and fifty times that of an incandescent lightbulb.

LEDs are not actually a new technology; they've been around for decades in the form of indicator lights in stereos and other equipment. More recently, LEDs were adopted for traffic signals because they lower energy costs and require less upkeep. They are also finding their way into other applications, such as computer monitors. For architectural purposes, the main issue with LEDs has for years involved the need to improve the quality of white light. Technological advancements have led to two ways of producing white light and even the ability to adjust color temperature (e.g., for the time of day) with LED fixtures. As with fluorescent lighting, warm whites are less efficacious than cold whites.

Current barriers to widespread LED adoption for lighting applications are cost and brightness. The costs of LED fixtures will undoubtedly decrease as production increases and the technology becomes less cutting-edge. In a pattern evocative of Moore's law, increases in light output are announced every few months.[13] As development advances, LEDs are opening up new possibilities in

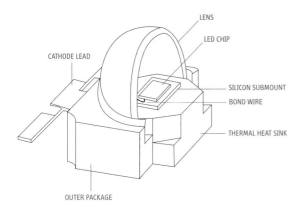

LENS

LED CHIP

CATHODE LEAD

SILICON SUBMOUNT

BOND WIRE

THERMAL HEAT SINK

OUTER PACKAGE

An LED is based on solid-state electronics and is a fundamentally different type of light source than incandescents and gas-based lamps (adapted from engerystar.gov).

lighting. Not only will conventional fixtures be retrofitted with LEDs—that's happening already—but new lighting typologies will emerge: designs that could not be created with older light sources.

LEDs have the potential to provide an energy efficient replacement for applications that fluorescents do not handle well. Fluorescents are effective at producing distributed light, not directed or focused light. Therefore, we still rely mainly on incandescent and halogen light for directed light. LEDs may allow us to retire most types of filament-based lighting once and for all.

But what about distributed light? For that there's another game-changing technology on the horizon: organic light emitting diodes (OLEDs). This is not the same "organic" as in organic foods—you won't be able to eat an OLED, nor will they biodegrade. Organic in this context refers to the underlying chemical structure of an OLED, based on organic compounds, in contrast to the silicon cells used in LEDs. The big difference between OLEDs and LEDs is that the former are produced as sheets of light-producing material, instead of as points of light. That means that, once the two technologies mature, we will have energy-efficient, non-mercury-consuming sources for both direct and distributed light, that is, viable replacements for both fluorescent and incandescent lightbulbs.

LEDs and OLEDs are not perfect solutions. They require energy to produce, and they use assorted materials, some of which are toxic. They also have end-of-life issues. A life cycle analysis (LCA), as we will explore in "Labels and Ratings: Measuring Ecodesign," is needed to determine just how advantageous they are compared to incandescents and fluorescents.

Concurrent with rapid advances in lighting technology, new building codes and regulations are being put in place as well. The Energy Independence and Security Act of 2007 phases in new efficacy requirements for lamps, which will, in effect, ban most common incandescent lamps between 2012 and 2014 (the European Union has already begun a phaseout). An even stricter set of requirements will take effect around 2020. It's important to note that this is not

The LED fixtures that make up this composition of three pendants could not have been made—at least not as elegantly—with other light sources.

OLED is a cutting-edge technology that is just beginning to find its way into light-fixture design. Here is a Philips prototype for an LED pendant.

a ban on incandescent lamps, but a ban on low-efficacy lamps regardless of the light source. In fact, some modified halogen lamps, designed to look like standard incandescents, are able to meet the new efficacy requirements, but it's highly unlikely they will be able to achieve the second-level requirements. All of the major lamp manufacturers are focusing on the development of LED and OLED products.

Lighting Controls

There is one way to save energy with incandescents, as well as with other light sources: by using dimmers and other controls. In most cases, the controls do not increase a lamp's efficacy; they just reduce the amount of energy they use. A dimmer does this by reducing wattage (which reduces brightness) when the light is in use, while a timer or other sensor cuts down on the length of time the light stays on.

Manual dimmers require user interaction, and it's not clear how often people actually dim their lights. Timers and sensors, on the other hand, work on their own. Occupancy sensors, which have improved in recent years, detect the presence of people, even without motion, so you can be less concerned about lights turning off, for example, while you're relaxing in the bathtub. Other types of sensors are able to determine how much natural light is in a space and whether to dim or turn the light off when it's not needed (in effect, harvesting daylight).

Localized lighting controls can be beneficial both in terms of energy efficiency and personal comfort. The ability to independently control individual workspace lighting will save energy, and it may increase productivity and improve employee well-being. This will be discussed in greater detail in the next chapter, "Indoor Environmental Quality."

Whole house control systems, however, are where the action is not only because they're high-tech and cool, but also because they offer opportunities for significant energy savings. From an ecological point of view, flashy effects—such as an Austin Powers–like button that dims the lights

This conference room is designed to maximize the harvesting of daylight by using controls to dim or turn off fixtures in areas with ample daylight.

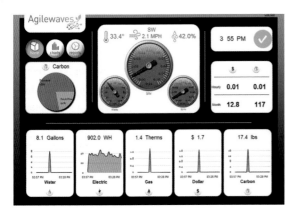

"Smart panels," or "building dashboards," allow monitoring of building performance, including electricity, gas, and water consumption.

and opens a fully stocked bar—are less interesting than, for example, being able to turn off lights and equipment from the front door as you leave. For ecogeeks, user-friendly tools that reduce energy consumption are as alluring as window shades that close by remote control.

As the smart grid is rolled out, it will enable new appliances and other energy-consuming devices to respond to peak demand and pricing. For instance, a dishwasher may be set to run when the electricity rates are lowest. New monitoring systems, for both offices and homes, provide readouts that tell you how much energy you're using or saving and where the energy is being consumed. Informational tools like these can be at least as important as high-efficiency technologies, because they engage people in efforts to save energy.

Daylighting

We do, of course, have another source of light: the sun. It has some distinct advantages and one notable disadvantage over electric lighting. The first advantage is that sunlight is pleasing to the senses. The second advantage is that, at least in moderation, it is healthy for you. It can help people feel and perform better. Though it may not exactly be a gauge of well-being, studies of Wal-Mart and other stores have shown that daylighting (usually via skylights) can have a significant effect—up to a 40 percent increase—on retail sales.[14] Studies of office workers have also shown significant productivity improvements in daylit spaces.[15] The third advantage is that sunlight is free. The notable disadvantage: nighttime.

There are a number of ways to utilize daylight; windows and skylights are the most obvious. One approach to maximizing daylight is to design shallow floor plates so that all interior spaces are close to windows. Daylight from windows can also be maximized through the use of reflective surfaces that transmit the light farther into the building. The most common of these is a light shelf, a light-colored horizontal surface near the top of a window that bounces light toward the ceiling, reflecting it farther into the space. Light shelves can double as *brises-soleils* or

The light shelf placed at the upper portion of the windows reflects daylight up to the ceiling, providing illumination deep into the space.

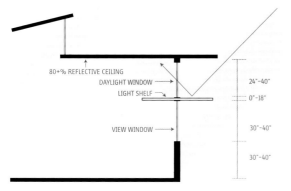

80+% REFLECTIVE CEILING
DAYLIGHT WINDOW →   24"–40"
LIGHT SHELF ↘   0"–18"
VIEW WINDOW →   30"–40"
     30"–40"

Light shelves may be indoors, outdoors, or both and may double as shading solutions. Clerestories can also bring light deeper into spaces.

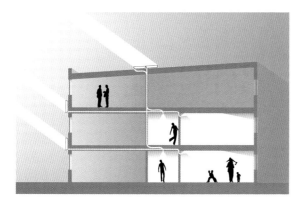

Collectors on the roof or facade focus light into fiber-optic tubes that are then run to light points where needed.

sun louvers to simultaneously shade a room from summer heat gain.

Another tool, variously known as a light tube, solar pipe, or tubular skylight, is a tube that conveys light from an aperture in the roof to a space below, for locations where skylights are not feasible. Fiber optics, tiny glass or plastic fibers along which light can be transmitted, can also be used to bring light to landlocked spaces. Fiber optics work with any light source, but as an eco-application, the idea is to place a daylight collector outside and then use the fibers to distribute the light elsewhere within the building. There are several advantages to fiber-optic lighting: there is no heat at the point of illumination, it does not rely on electricity (if sunlight is the source), UV light is not transmitted, and it requires little or no maintenance.

The use of features like light shelves, clerestories (high windows), light-colored materials, and solar tubes to bring daylight farther into buildings and reduce the need for electric lighting, especially when combined with daylight sensors, constitutes daylight harvesting. What could be more sustainable than using a readily available, renewable, and free resource in place of energy from fossil fuels?

Energy Modeling

Knowing what steps are available for energy efficiency is really only useful if you can predict results and cost-effectiveness.[16] Energy modeling is the best way to accomplish this. Once complex and daunting, the process is now more accessible to designers, thanks to new software and the evolution of building information modeling (BIM).

The general premise of energy modeling is to predict a building's energy consumption based on its design and then use the information to improve the design. Most software programs start by asking for basic project information, such as location and use. Then they either require you to create a model within the program or allow you to make use of an existing building model. For instance, Google SketchUp add-ons can evaluate what you have created in (or exported to) SketchUp, and Autodesk has a program called Ecotect Analysis for modeling energy within

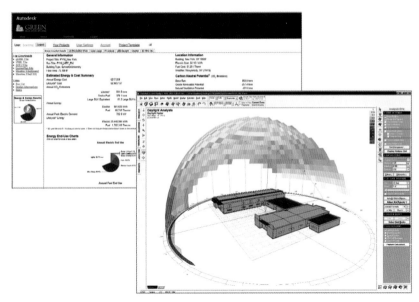

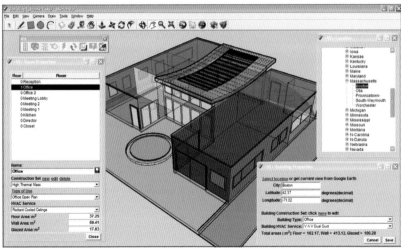

Screenshots from Autodesk's Ecotect Analysis and Integrated Environmental
Solutions' SketchUp plug-in.

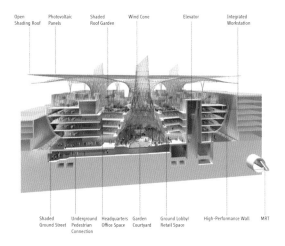

Open Shading Roof | Photovoltaic Panels | Shaded Roof Garden | Wind Cone | Elevator | Integrated Workstation

Shaded Ground Street | Underground Pedestrian Connection | Headquarters Office Space | Garden Courtyard | Ground Lobby/ Retail Space | High-Performance Wall | MRT

designs created from their applications or other BIM software. Depending on the complexity of the program, the model may be simple or a fairly complete representation.

As critical as energy efficiency is, it is important to view it as only one criterion of ecological design. The design of a structure must be approached holistically: a building should be conceived as a system, with consideration given to other environmental and social criteria. The next chapter looks at some of these criteria by examining how buildings affect their human occupants.

Masdar Headquarters, outside Abu Dhabi, designed by Adrian Smith + Gordon Gill Architecture, will interweave passive and active energy efficiency.

Indoor Environ- mental Quality

In the 1960s and 1970s, the nascent ecology movement focused public attention on visible pollution, which led to the Clean Air Act of 1963 and the Clean Water Act of 1972. These had major impacts not only on the quality of air and water, but also on our attitudes toward pollution, reflecting a fundamental change in priorities. This set the stage for political and public acceptance of environmentalism.

What this legislation did not address, however, was air quality *inside* buildings. This was less of an issue when building envelopes were not as airtight, and outdoor air mixed more freely with indoor air. In the past, buildings dealt with indoor air quality (IAQ) by default, unintentionally employing the old (and inadequate) adage "The solution to pollution is dilution." Fresh air entered buildings largely by infiltration through gaps at doors and windows and through poorly insulated walls and roofs. Contemporary energy-conserving construction methods and products dramatically reduce infiltration, in turn making controlled ventilation necessary.

Ventilation is typically measured by how often the air in a space is exchanged with fresh air, rated in air changes per hour (ACH). Deficient rates of air change, resulting in "stale" air, can create health problems, even without the presence of two common exacerbating factors. One is the addition of more and more synthetic or toxic materials to our interiors in the forms of finishes, sealants, textiles, other materials, and cleansers. The synergistic effect of these chemicals in combination with the presence of bacteria, mold, dust, etc., that can accumulate in an under-ventilated space amounts to a chemical cocktail. Studies conducted by the National Institute for Occupational Safety and Health in the 1990s found that 24 percent of IAQ problems are attributable to these combined causes.[1]

On average, the typical American will spend 90 percent of his or her life indoors. The implication of this evolution from our pre–Industrial Revolution lifestyles is that improving outdoor air quality is crucial, but it may be less significant to human health than the need to improve IAQ.

These factors have sometimes led to a condition called sick building syndrome, in which occupants

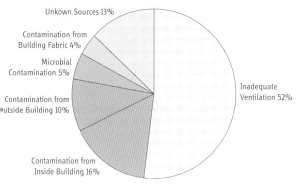

Unkown Sources 13%

Contamination from Building Fabric 4%

Microbial Contamination 5%

Contamination from Outside Building 10%

Inadequate Ventilation 52%

Contamination from Inside Building 16%

Sources of IAQ contamination (adapted from OSHA).

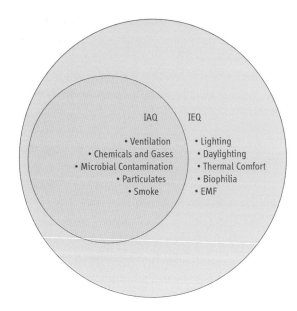

IAQ   IEQ

• Ventilation   • Lighting
• Chemicals and Gases   • Daylighting
• Microbial Contamination   • Thermal Comfort
• Particulates   • Biophilia
• Smoke   • EMF

IAQ is concerned only with air quality. IEQ looks at all factors that bear on the occupants' well-being.

experience acute health and comfort effects that appear to be linked to time spent in a building, but no specific illness or cause can be identified.[2] In severe cases, buildings have been completely gutted to eliminate the causes. Many experts also suspect that multiple chemical sensitivity, a condition in which people become acutely sensitive to environmental factors, is caused by exposure to that chemical cocktail.

The health effects related to IAQ are not subjective, nor are they just about feeling better. There are serious financial implications in terms of medical costs, lost work time, and—perhaps most significant—lost productivity in the workplace, amounting to a loss of $60 billion annually in the United States.[3]

IAQ is determined by indoor air pollutants. There are additional factors that contribute to the general well-being of a building's users, including lighting, thermal comfort, and connection to nature. Combined with IAQ, these comprise the broader topic of indoor environmental quality (IEQ). Again, these are not just feel-good ideas; they have real, quantifiable effects. For instance, schoolchildren learn faster in classrooms that are well lit and provide outdoor views; manufacturing defects decrease with good lighting and the use of daylighting in factories; and employee turnover (a significant business expense) diminishes in settings where employees are physically more comfortable and able to maintain some control over their work environment.

Indoor Toxics

The medical precept "First, do no harm" could easily have an ethical equivalent in architecture. If our primary responsibility as a profession is to ensure the safety of a building's occupants, it stands to reason that we should not specify materials that could cause deleterious effects. In the modern, chemical-laden world, the list of ingredients, both synthetic and natural, that can harm people is long and includes asbestos, formaldehyde, lead, mercury, polyvinyl chloride (PVC), volatile organic compounds (VOCs), radon, dust, bacteria, viruses, mold, and funguses. Some of these, such as dust and other human-borne contaminants, are unavoidable; the remedies are ventilation, filtration, and limiting the use of surfaces that can retain them, like carpets. Other elements can be minimized by not installing them in a project. In most of the developed world, asbestos and lead are either banned or regulated. VOCs, which are frequently found in paints, adhesives, and finishes, can be minimized by specifying low- or non-VOC products. The use of PVC (often referred to as "vinyl") is more controversial, as the vinyl industry maintains that it is a harmless and environmentally preferable alternative. Meanwhile, environmentalists say its production process endangers factory workers, it emits lethal dioxin when burned, and it leaches toxic additives when left in landfills.

Solids like asbestos and lead are harmful when they break off into pieces that can be inhaled or ingested. Other chemicals, such as VOCs, get released into the air in a process called off-gassing or out-gassing. Some release fairly quickly, which means that one approach to using them is to allow time for off-gassing prior to occupancy, during which the building is ventilated and sometimes heated to hasten the process. A better approach, of course, is to avoid using these materials altogether.

A useful resource when evaluating the relative toxicity of a material is the Material Safety and Data Sheet (MSDS). The U.S. Department of Labor's Occupational Safety and Health Administration (OSHA) requires manufacturers to publish an MSDS for all materials containing known hazardous ingredients. The hitch is in the word *known*; if the hazard is not established or recognized by the government or is being debated, its inclusion in an MSDS is not required.

This would not necessarily be the case in Europe, where the precautionary principle has been adopted. In the United States, environmental regulations are not usually put in place until all evidence is in. In Europe, the burden of proof falls in the opposite direction: in the absence of scientific consensus, a risk-mitigating preventive approach is taken, and the policy is to err on the safe side while awaiting more conclusive evidence. The

Elimination of toxic chemicals—in adhesives, paints, and cabinetry and floor finishes, among other products—is one of the primary steps in addressing IAQ.

American approach favors commerce—never mind that an impending liability may not be in the long-term interest of a business—while the European standard favors safety. This dichotomy plays out in several environmental areas, including climate change, materials safety, and food safety.[4] Just because American policy tends toward the wait-and-see approach doesn't mean we should apply the same thinking to design. Doesn't it make sense to avoid something altogether if there is a chance it will incur a problem or create some danger? It's common sense to take out fire insurance even if, odds are, you probably won't have a fire. Think of the precautionary principle as insurance or, better yet, just good business practice. If asbestos regulations had been implemented earlier, in a precautionary way, not only would lives have been saved, but the companies involved might not have been forced out of business under the weight of litigation.

Thermal Comfort

We're all familiar with the complaint at home or in the office that one person is chilly while another is hot. Not only does this lead to heated debates, but it can also cause physical discomfort, low morale, and diminished productivity in the workplace. One solution, in offices at least, is to provide local thermal controls. Some HVAC systems are more flexible in this regard than others. One of the most flexible is underfloor air distribution (UFAD), in which

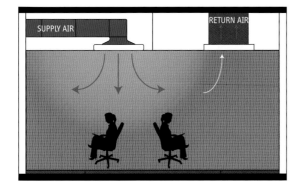

These two diagrams compare a conventional HVAC distribution system (left) with an UFAD system.

The grilles from this UFAD system are easily accessible so office workers can adjust their local environment.

heated or cooled air is distributed below a raised floor, alongside wiring for electrical and data systems. Because the system's air-distribution points are located at floor level, rather than on the ceiling, they are accessible to occupants and readily adjusted. Additional advantages of UFAD include the fact that the air flows closer to where it's needed (rather than being pushed from the ceiling or perimeter) and, because of the flexibility and simplicity of access, it is easier to alter or renovate the space as needs change. The more localized flow of air results in less discomfort caused by moving air, as well as diminished circulation of allergens and pollutants.

Window treatments also have a role. Properly utilized, they can significantly improve the passive solar properties of a building. Of more relevance to IEQ, though, they can reduce glare and prevent overheating while preserving views. Having an outdoor view, although not part of thermal comfort, plays an important role in IEQ and is one component of how we relate to the natural world.

Biophilia

Environmentalism is often miscast as a back-to-nature movement. Part of the legacy that sustainable design contends with is the assumption that it requires an almost transcendental asceticism and communing with nature (like Henry David Thoreau's simple living experiment at Walden Pond). On the contrary, ecological footprint analyses indicate that dense urban living actually treads more lightly on the land than directly living off it.

The theory of biophilia, as put forward by biologist Edward O. Wilson, would seem to be in opposition to urbanism. He proffers that we have an innate or subconscious need to bond with other living systems, suggesting that we are not at our best in isolation from nature.[5] As an urbanite, I've often wondered how true this is. Are cities unnatural? Can you bond with nature in the asphalt jungle? The answer, I suspect, is that everyone is different and that our individual bonds with nature are very personal. Some people find cities stifling; others are more like Eva Gabor in the 1960s television series *Green Acres*.

An application of biophilia, the recently completed Guardian Angel's Hospital, designed by Emilio Ambasz, incorporates a planted courtyard to enhance patient recovery.

Urbanites notwithstanding, the effects of biophilia are real. Dogs can calm people who have nervous conditions, and bedridden hospital patients with window views of natural scenery recover faster. It stands to reason, therefore, that vistas, landscaped courtyards, and other elements that break the barrier between inside and outside are good for our health.

Air Filtration

But do the effects of indoor landscaping go beyond biophilia and improving mental health? For example, do indoor plants actually clean the air? The National Aeronautics and Space Administration (NASA) conducted a study to see if plants could assist with air purification in space stations, and they determined that plants do in fact filter air. Some are better at filtering than others, however, and it would take *a lot* of plants to have any significant effect on IAQ. There's also the issue that indoor plants or their soils may have negative effects on allergy sufferers.

This trade-off emphasizes an important fact about sustainable design, one that reappears in many forms: there is never a perfect answer. There are no perfect green designs, except perhaps building nothing at all, which is usually not an option. It may sound defeatist—and contrary to my earlier critique that the incremental less-bad approach is inadequate—but the reality is we must examine the trade-offs of every decision we make while searching for the deepest achievable shade of green.

IEQ comes down to general well-being and how people feel. It can be subjective and individualized, hence the emphasis on tools such as local adjustability of HVAC and lighting. Allowing people to modify their environment both increases comfort and provides a sense of individual control. However, there is a continual tug-of-war between creating airtight, environmentally controlled interiors and the need to provide ample fresh air. Depending on the building's function and its occupants, air exchangers may suffice, but the air they bring in is only as fresh as the outdoor supply. When combined with indoor contaminants, it may need treatment beyond the limited amount that, according to NASA, plants can provide. In those cases, filtration systems are needed. For filtration of particulate matter such as dust, smoke, pollen, animal dander, mold, bacteria, and viruses, the most common method is a mechanical filter, essentially a fine screen. These are rated in minimum efficiency reporting values (MERVs) ranging from 1 to 20. A higher rating is preferable and indicates that the screen is able to filter out smaller particles. High efficiency particulate air (HEPA) filters have MERV ratings exceeding 16. Other types of filters remove gaseous pollutants (e.g., vehicle exhaust, cleaning product fumes, and finishes) through methods such as activated charcoal, but these are used less commonly, particularly in homes.

Previous chapters discussed concepts for saving money by consuming less water and energy and for diminishing demand on our ecosystems; in effect, these chapters addressed two parts of the triple bottom line: planet and profit. With IEQ, however, the emphasis shifts to the third bottom line: *people*. The three bottom lines, as indicated by the Venn diagram that usually depicts them (see page 20), often overlap. Improving the people bottom line, as I've noted, can also improve the financial, or profit, bottom line for both businesses and families.

Plants and IEQ
Top Ten Plants Most Effective in Removing Formaldehyde, Benzene, and Carbon Monoxide from the Air
Bamboo Palm (Chamaedorea Seifritzii)
Chinese Evergreen (Aglaonema Modestum)
English Ivy (Hedera Helix)
Gerbera Daisy (Gerbera Jamesonii)
Janet Craig (Dracaena "Janet Craig")
Marginata (Dracaena Marginata)
Mass Cane/Corn Plant (Dracaena Massangeana)
Mother-in-Law's Tongue (Sanseveiera Laurentii)
Pot Mum (Chrysantheium morifolium)
Peace Lily (Spathiphyllus)
Warneckii (Dracaena "Warneckii")

A NASA study identified these plants as having higher potential for indoor air purification.

Materials

Typical Construction Waste for a 2,000 sq. ft. Home	
Material	Weight (in lbs.)
Solid Sawn Wood	1,600
Engineered Wood	1,400
Drywall	2,000
Cardboard	600
Metals	150
Vinyl (PVC)*	150
Masonry*	1,000
Containers (Paints, Caulks, etc.)	50
Other	1,050
Total	8,000

*Typical house is assumed to have a front brick facade and three facades of vinyl siding.

This table lists the on-site construction waste from a typical residence (adapted from NAHB).

After energy efficiency, perhaps the topic most associated with ecodesign is recycling: is a building or product made out of recycled materials? This was an even bigger factor in the early days of environmentalism when there was a greater focus on the three Rs, and it remains among the primary criteria of sustainability. However, recycled content is just one consideration in the environmental selection of a material.

An enormous amount of the planet's resources is consumed in the construction of buildings. The numbers are staggering. Even more disturbing is that much of it ends up as construction debris, thrown out before it has even been used.[1] Combine that with other factors—the sometimes short life spans of buildings, worldwide population growth, and the rapidly developing economies of China and India—and it becomes obvious that we need to take a closer look at the amounts and types of materials we select and how we use them.

Most of this discussion will center on the ecosystem implications of our material choices: how to sustainably utilize materials within the finite, closed-loop capacity of the Earth, how to use less energy to make these materials, and how to use and waste less material in general. But a materials discussion should perhaps start with health, as in avoiding materials that are toxic or harmful to people or ecosystems. Some of these materials were reviewed in regards to indoor air quality, but it is also necessary to evaluate materials in terms of the dangers posed by their acquisition, fabrication, and disposal. For example, asbestos is dangerous to miners and fabricators as well as building occupants. PVC is as controversial in its production and end-of-life phases as it is when installed. Mercury exposure can result from handling broken fluorescent bulbs or in their improper disposal in landfills, but far greater exposure arises from the production of electricity through burning coal. A significant percentage of that electricity is utilized in the extraction, harvesting, and fabrication of materials.

These realities emphasize the importance of examining the impacts of materials throughout their life cycles, from acquisition through usage, disposal, and recycling.

Dematerialization

One way to look at materials is in terms of consumption, which brings us back to the reduce part of the three Rs mantra. Reducing the amount of material in a structure can involve building more efficiently, designing to use materials more efficiently, or just making smaller buildings and spaces (as discussed in "Site Issues"). The resulting decrease in materials usage is known as dematerialization. In industrial design, it's often called lightweighting.

Prefabrication has received a lot of attention in recent years as a more efficient method of construction; fabrication in the contained and controlled environment of a factory has advantages over exposed construction on site. Interest in prefabs has waxed and waned over time. In the first half of the twentieth century, Sears catalog houses and Fuller's futuristic Dymaxion House brought prefab into the public eye. Today, there's a proliferation of green prefabs, often produced by architects. The excitement has frequently outpaced the reality, in part because people expect prefab construction to be less expensive and then turn away when they discover it often isn't.

Offsite production does have benefits. Since everything except the foundation is constructed indoors, materials are not subjected to poor weather or pilferage, and recycling of scraps is simpler. In an assembly-line process, materials usage can be streamlined and quality control may be tighter. However, there is some question as to whether these gains are offset by the need to transport the finished assembly. It's not necessarily the carbon footprint of the transportation that is at issue. (In conventional construction, the raw materials are transported to the site, so the difference is probably close to a wash.) Moving the assembled structures often requires additional protection and reinforcing, resulting in packaging waste once the building is "unwrapped" on site. That waste can sometimes offset the materials efficiency of the factory assembly.

A way around this quandary is to prefabricate parts of the building, which are then assembled on site, rather than shipping a completed structure. This is often referred to as modular construction; both the Sears homes and the

Prefabricated construction has been through several cycles of popularity and economic success: a Sears home (top) and Buckminster Fuller's Wichita House (1946).

Desert House (2005) in Desert Hot Springs, California, designed by
Marmol Radziner, is a prototype prefab home.

Koby Cottage (2009), designed by Garrison Architects, is a contemporary example of a prefab home (shown in factory).

SIPs have thermal as well as material and transportation advantages.

A thermographic image of a conventional frame house clearly shows each stud, indicating a thermal bridge. Without studs, SIPs have much less thermal transmission.

These framing models, by EHDD Architecture, show that advanced framing techniques (also called optimum value engineering) can result in the use of 25 percent less wood.

Dymaxion concept are examples. Structural insulated panels (SIPs), a prefab method for wood buildings that offers a number of green attributes, fall into this category. SIPs are sandwiches of foam surrounded by a wood composite sheathing material called oriented strand board (OSB). The panels are prefabricated to precise sizes in the factory and then raised on site to form the building exterior. Because the panels are shipped flat, sitting on top of one another, they require both less packaging and less space than assembled prefab structures. From a thermal point of view, the building envelope is much tighter than one produced by conventional frame construction, because the panels are more airtight and do not have thermal bridges (there are no studs to conduct heat from the exterior materials to the interior).

Framing, too, can be dematerialized. The technique known as advanced framing, or optimum value engineering, reduces the amount of wood needed to frame a building. In advanced framing, 2x6 studs are used instead of 2x4s, and they are spaced at twenty-four inches on center rather than sixteen. This not only saves materials but also decreases labor and increases insulation. (The thicker wall cavity is filled with more insulation and has fewer thermal bridges.) Advanced framing also employs more efficient details, such as corners made of two studs rather than three and alignment of members so that plates and headers can be reduced. Efficient dimensioning, through which design is based on the precut, off-the-shelf sizes of standard lumber, can be an element of advanced framing and may result in significantly less waste from cutoffs. These techniques can reduce framing materials by more than 20 percent.

Other forms of dematerialization may involve design or structural concepts. These may be very visible, a result of unconventional design, or invisible, as in the case of framing methods. Fuller gave us an early example in his geodesic dome, which remains one of the most materials-efficient ways to enclose a volume with no interior structure. Foster + Partners' Hearst Tower (2006) is another example: the exposed triangular structural grid is not

The unusual form of the Hearst Tower (2006), designed by Foster + Partners, uses 20 percent less steel than a conventional steel tower.

merely aesthetic. It reportedly uses 20 percent less structural steel (or a savings of about two thousand tons) than a regular steel frame would have.

Reclaimed Materials

Next to using nothing, reusing a material is usually the ecologically best option. This is pretty obvious: if the material already exists (having been made for a previous use), we don't have to mine, grow, or fabricate it. As a further benefit, reusing materials keeps them out of the waste stream. It's a very Spaceship Earth–minded concept: use what we have rather than throwing it out and making more.

Some types of reclaimed materials—such as wide-plank flooring and vintage hardware—are sought after, but too often there is a stigma attached to used materials. Our culture fosters a newer-is-better belief and tends to shun things that belonged to someone else. But the combination of environmental goals, cost savings, and aesthetics (think of how popular distressed materials have become) is strengthening the case and increasing the demand for reclaimed materials. New businesses, some charitable and some for-profit, are springing up where used construction materials—ranging from construction leftovers to used timbers, windows, cabinets, and appliances—can be donated (saving disposal fees) and purchased. And Craigslist-like websites now serve as brokers, connecting those who have materials for donation or sale with those looking to procure them.

In renovations, reclaimed materials can close the loop more tightly: rather than removing and disposing of materials, reinstalling results in cost savings as well as environmental benefits. You can reuse wood flooring, reinstall fixtures (if they are energy- or water-efficient), and convert old kitchen cabinets into storage units.

Recycled Materials

Recycled materials differ from reclaimed materials in that they have been put through reprocessing before beginning another usage. The reprocessing usually entails transportation and energy consumption, which explains why reuse

Homasote has been made from recycled newsprint since 1916.

These aluminum tiles are made from 100 percent postconsumer aluminum sourced from reclaimed aircraft parts.

is considered preferable to recycling. (Remember the order of the three Rs is reduce, reuse, and then recycle.)

A number of terms need to be clarified here. First, claiming a material is recyclable is not the same as claiming it is recycled. Recyclable just means that *if* the material gets separated from the waste stream and *if* it gets to a recycling facility, *then* it can be recycled. Recycled, on the other hand, means it already has been reprocessed. Ideally, a material is both.

Recycled materials can come from two types of sources. Postconsumer materials have been used and then sent for recycling. Postindustrial (also called preconsumer) materials are industrial waste, the scraps from the factory. Recycled denim insulation, mentioned in "Energy Efficiency: Passive Techniques," is a good example of an instance in which the two sources can be confused. Until recently, most of the insulation was not actually made from used jeans; it was from factory remnants.[2] This didn't necessarily make it less green: both sources represent materials savings and diversion from landfills.

Most recycling processes result in a loss of quality or value in the material. Every time paper is recycled, for example, the fibers become shorter, yielding a lower grade of paper. In a technical sense, then, the paper has not been recycled but has been downcycled. Aluminum, on the other hand, can be recycled with little loss in value. Examples of upcycling, creating materials that have a higher value after reprocessing, are much harder to come by. The definition is also a bit tricky. If a plastic bottle is shredded and made into a fleece jacket, which has greater value than the bottle, is that upcycling? Or is it downcycled because the plastic itself has been degraded and may no longer be recyclable for future uses? If we use the latter criteria, which considers the flow of the materials as opposed to the products made from the materials, there's a strong argument that *materials* upcycling is not possible because it violates the laws of thermodynamics. *Products*, however, may be termed upcycled. In fact, most products, whether made of recycled materials or not, have more value than their component materials (or they wouldn't be worth producing).

Recycled glass bottles are used to make other products, such as kitchen counters (top).

In designating products upcycled, we also need to differentiate between upcycling and "upusing." A product that takes salvage materials and makes them into something more valuable is actually upused, not upcycled, since the materials have not been reprocessed. The real issue here, from the point of view of ecology and materials and energy flows, is not whether the new product has more value, but whether the component materials are being used in a closed loop with minimal waste of resources and energy.[3]

Two additional notes: It's important to be aware of the percentage of recycled content. A material can be labeled recycled if it has any recycled content at all, but obviously a higher percentage is better, and a very low percentage can be irrelevant and misleading. If the percentage isn't apparent, ask.

A complication occurs when a recycled material is blended into a composite such as a resin. When that happens, it becomes difficult or impossible to separate the materials afterward for re-recycling. So while the composite may have recycled content, it wouldn't be recyclable.

Embodied Energy

Another reason the recycling rate of aluminum is so high is that it takes much less energy (and therefore less expense) to make recycled aluminum than it does to make original (or virgin) material—about 95 percent less. The energy that goes into making something—acquiring its raw materials, producing it, and transporting it—is called embodied energy. A material's embodied energy is a factor in determining how green a material is. Wood has a very low embodied energy level because nature has done most of the work for us. All we have to do is cut it, transport it, and mill it. Virgin aluminum, by contrast, is at the other end of the scale. The processes of mining, refining, smelting, and fabricating, along with transporting, make it one of our most energy-intensive materials.

Petroleum-based plastics actually have a fairly low embodied energy compared with energy-intense materials such as metals, but that doesn't take into account the feedstock: the petroleum that is the raw material for the

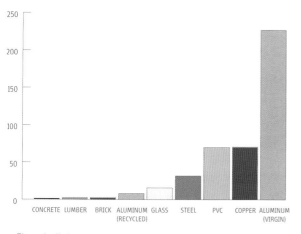

The embodied energy of some typical construction materials (adapted from Architecture 2030).

plastics. And while concrete also has a fairly low embodied energy, the Portland cement in a standard concrete mix uses a lot of heat in its production process. Fortunately, we have a good alternative: substituting fly ash for part of the cement. Fly ash, as explained in "Energy Efficiency: Active Techniques," is a residue from the burning of coal. As 50 percent of U.S. electricity is produced from burning coal, we have a lot of fly ash, creating a huge disposal issue. Substituting what is essentially a zero-embodied-energy material for one with high embodied energy and simultaneously solving a waste problem are together another example of a win-win solution. Up to 40 percent of the cement in a concrete mix can be switched for fly ash. This can reduce the embodied energy of the concrete by nearly 40 percent, since almost all of the energy used to make concrete is due to the cement. There are additional benefits. Concrete made with fly ash is actually stronger than conventional concrete. Furthermore, fly ash contains trace mercury, and if the ash is left for landfills (or worse, as in the case of the 2008 Tennessee spill), the mercury can get into our ecosystems. But when it is used in concrete, the mercury becomes inertly embedded.[4]

In our globalized economy, many materials travel long distances, from their extraction to the places where they're processed and fabricated and then to the construction site. The resulting fuel consumption makes transportation a significant component of some materials' embodied energy (in addition to incurring other transportation issues, such as air pollution and greenhouse gas emissions). An obvious solution is to buy locally sourced and locally produced materials, but this isn't necessarily simple. It used to be that regional architecture might be characterized by use of a local stone or wood. This was largely born of necessity, due to the difficulty and expense of transportation. Though stone may still be quarried locally (if it hasn't been quarried out), it may have been shipped to other parts of the world for forming into slabs and polishing. Determining what constitutes local sourcing is not always straightforward.

Renewable Materials

The fact that stone sources get quarried out illustrates that some materials are renewable and others aren't. Put more accurately, some materials are more quickly renewable than others. Even oil is renewable, albeit at a glacial pace. (That may be an unfortunate description, given the rate at which many glaciers are receding.) The problem is that we are consuming oil far faster than the Earth makes it.

In a Spaceship Earth sustainability scenario, we would not consume anything faster than it can be replaced by nature or by us. We can't make oil or granite, but we do have materials that we grow or that are made from things we grow. These are known collectively as biobased materials, and they range from trees to cotton to bioplastics.

Biobased materials are not free of ecological issues: they can be overharvested, grown with chemical assistance, consume too much water, or compete with food production. A truly green renewable material would be sustainably harvested and organically grown, utilize indigenous species, and not be planted at the expense of food crops.

Bamboo is a good case study. It's not merely renewable; it's rapidly renewable, unlike most trees that take generations to grow. However, the demand has grown so quickly that it has outpaced the capacity of sustainable harvesting practices, and we are seeing forests cleared for bamboo plantations. Monocrop plantations are not sustainable ecosystems. They uproot natural systems, forcing out or killing off wildlife, and replace the balanced ecosystems with industrial agriculture that depletes nutrients and requires fertilizers and pesticides. And those aren't the only issues. Most bamboo is grown in Asia, so it must be transported long distances to reach the U.S. market, increasing its embodied energy and carbon footprint. Furthermore, until recently all bamboo boards used adhesives that contained formaldehyde.

So is bamboo a sustainable material? As with many environmental questions, it depends. In part because bamboo is a grass, not a tree, there were few ecocertifications for it until the Forest Stewardship Council (FSC) began certifying bamboo production in 2008. FSC certification is an

Bamboo is a rapidly renewable and very strong material, but increased demand is resulting in unsustainable monocrop bamboo plantations.

Clear-cutting of forests results in ecosystem disruption, including displacement or loss of animals and vulnerability to mudslides. Replanting with a single tree species does not recreate a functioning ecosystem.

intense process, because it involves what's called chain of custody, tracking the material through its stages from forest to mill to lumberyard to cabinet shop.[5]

FSC certification is part of the push for sustainable forestry. Conventional forestry employs clear-cutting, in which entire swaths are cut and cleared simply because it is a less expensive method. Forests do need to regenerate: old trees die, compost, and provide soil, nutrients, and space for new growth. Natural forest fires, too, are a part of that process. But when a forest is clear-cut, it cannot regenerate normally. It takes much longer, endangering wildlife and possibly incurring mudslides in the interim.

While clear-cutting is the issue in the northern hemisphere, slash-and-burn farming is rapidly diminishing our equatorial rainforests. The bulk of this practice is related to clearing land for farm and grazing uses, but demand for rainforest woods exacerbates the problem. While there are certifications, including the FSC's, for tropical woods, many rainforest advocates say the certifications are often weak or circumvented. They maintain that it is better not to specify rainforest woods at all.

Plastic is an evil word to most environmentalists. On the acquisition side, plastics are generally petroleum based. In the usage phase, they may contain chemicals that are dangerous to humans and other species and, when they are thrown away, they do not break down for hundreds of years (at least). This accumulation, by the way, does not occur only in landfills. There is an area twice the size of Texas in the middle of the Pacific Ocean known as the Pacific Gyre—or, more descriptively, as the Great Pacific Garbage Patch—in which untold tons of plastic are trapped in circular currents. It's been called the largest landfill in the world.

Plastics weren't always made from petroleum, though. The very first plastic, invented in 1855, was made from plant cellulose. A famous 1941 photo of Henry Ford shows him swinging an axe at a car trunk made from a mixture of plant materials in order to show its superior strength (and lower weight) compared with steel. After World War II, synthetic plastics became cheaper and bioplastic development fell by the wayside, but now there is renewed interest and

Henry Ford was enamored with bioplastics. Here he is demonstrating that the bioplastic trunk of his car can resist a blow from an axe.

plastics are being produced from several types of plants. Corn-based plastics are probably the most commercially developed. Planting crops for biobased materials, however, can compete with other agriculture, specifically food farming. The demand for corn for ethanol has already driven up the price of corn as well as other crops. Adding to that demand is not an effective path. It's far better to use non-food plants or, better still, to use the plant parts left over after the food has been harvested. Plastic is being made, for example, from bagasse, which is the residue from sugarcane harvesting. There are other materials produced from "free" agricultural by-products. Wheatboard, though not a plastic, is a sustainable alternative building material made from the stalks of wheat, which would otherwise be plowed under or burned.

There are two more issues concerning bioplastics and, in fact, any plant-based material. The first has to do with whether it is organically farmed, or grown without chemical fertilizers and pesticides. Cotton is often billed as a natural material. Unless it is organic cotton, though, it has probably been grown using standard industrial methods, which lead to contaminated groundwater and downstream dead zones where aquatic life cannot exist. *Natural* is a misleading term that has no regulated definition. The word *organic*, on the other hand, is strictly defined.

A more difficult issue is the use of genetically modified organisms (GMOs). Most GMOs are probably safe, but there are concerns about unintended consequences, such as side effects on ecosystems (as well as on humans) and proliferation (GMOs overtaking other plants). There are also many positive aspects, both realized and potential, but the precautionary principle advises that we should proceed carefully with new technologies.

Bioplastics, along with many other biobased materials, may also be biodegradable, meaning they have the ability to break down into materials that can return to the land. These fall into the category of biological nutrients, described in "Ecodesign: What and Why." But as with many other ecological terms, the word *biodegradable* can be misleading or misapplied. Most materials will not break

Herman Miller's Mirra chair can be disassembled in fifteen minutes, and almost all of its parts are recyclable.

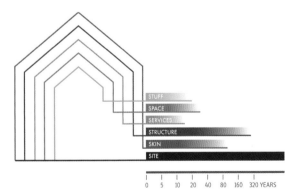

The "shearing layers" of a building were first described by Francis Duffy and then expanded by Stewart Brand and Tedd Benson. The life expectancy of the layers varies somewhat among the different analyses; this illustration uses a combination of their estimates.

down when buried in landfills. A biodegradable plastic—or a newspaper, for that matter—will remain virtually unchanged for many years unless it is exposed to the elements. Some materials require exposure to oxygen, while others require enzymes or bacteria.

Durability or Planned Obsolescence?

In light of the amount of material and embodied energy invested in every building, a clear element of sustainability is ensuring that it has a long life. With few exceptions (such as temporary structures), building for durability is one of the basic tenets of ecodesign. But creating a structure that will endure over the years is not just a matter of designing it with long-lasting materials. One perhaps obvious point: the building must be valued by those who use it. If the design does not result in a building that functions well and is pleasing, then it is likely to be renovated or demolished sooner.

If a building is to last, then it needs to be able to adapt to changes in usage, technology, and cultural patterns. In other words, it needs to be durable and flexible. "Design for deconstruction" is one way to achieve flexibility and provide for the eventual need to replace the building. The industrial design world has for a while been at work on design for disassembly (DfD, which can also stand for design for deconstruction). One high-profile example involves the office chair; several manufacturers have engaged in a kind of competition to design the chair that can be disassembled the fastest and with the fewest tools. The objective is to make recycling more economically viable by designing so that materials are readily separable at the end of the product's life.

Buildings, of course, are more complicated than office chairs. And they should last longer—or at least parts of them should. Stewart Brand, in *How Buildings Learn*, describes how buildings should be thought of as having six layers, ranging from the site, which is timeless, to the skin and structure, which may last generations, to furnishings that are frequently changed.[6]

The application of this concept has become known as open building, and it can lead to a fundamentally different

The Cellophane House (2008), designed by KieranTimberlake, can be disassembled, transported, and reassembled.

way of understanding buildings in which these layers are independent.[7] To a degree, modern offices do this already with non-load bearing, demountable partitions and mechanical cores. But more often than not, an office renovation or a home remodel involves brute force removal (destruction, really) of building materials. Imagine if the walls of our homes were built so that wiring and plumbing could be easily accessed for repairs and modifications—without cutting holes in walls, perhaps without encountering obstacles, and then without patching and painting (or, for instance, if windows could be replaced without entailing interior and exterior damage). The key lies in separating the layers so that the less durable layers can be altered without interfering with the others.

Open building also relates to the concept of future-proofing: designing and constructing buildings to anticipate the future. If, for instance, PV panels are not in the budget but may be added eventually, run conduits to the roof and provide support structure so that the panels and wiring can be accommodated later with minimal disruption and cost. Similarly, a gray-water system may not be allowed by current code, but if you provide the necessary plumbing at the outset, it can be implemented by simply opening a valve when the code catches up.

Eventually most buildings will reach the end of their useful lives. But because we don't design buildings to be taken apart, they usually face the wrecking ball method of demolition, which makes it extremely difficult to reclaim or recycle materials. One of the first rules of DfD is to assemble with mechanical fasteners rather than permanent connections, especially when joining dissimilar materials. KieranTimberlake's Loblolly House (2006) is an example of this technique. The house is made of a bolted-together steel frame with removable modules. The firm's prefab Cellophane House (2008) explores this concept further.

As materials become more valuable and green design takes hold, the field of demolition is being replaced by deconstruction, the goal of which is to keep materials out of the waste stream. To truly enable this will require rethinking many of our building systems, ranging from glue-down carpeting to plastic laminates to typical walls, in which metal or wood studs, wallboard, compound, paint, and other assorted materials are essentially bonded into a single composite.

Among the layers in the illustration, many building elements are often replaced within thirty years or less, some far less. This may be because they wear out, become outdated aesthetically or technologically, or become victims of the normal cycle of renovation. With these short-lived elements, it especially makes sense to plan for their end of life from the beginning. One very interesting approach is not to buy the material or product at all, but to lease it from the manufacturer, who then gets it back when it is removed or no longer needed. This concept, often called products of service, has long been employed for other circumstances, such as office copiers. With a copier, you don't really want to own the machine; you want the *service* of being able to make copies without the headaches and liabilities of ownership. A number of companies are looking at how this concept might be applied to buildings. The carpet company Interface experimented with it through its Evergreen Lease program, which was based on businesses leasing carpet tile and then returning the tile to Interface for recycling when they were through with it. The program, unfortunately, succumbed to bureaucratic inertia, as companies couldn't figure out whether the lease would be budgeted as capital improvements or operations and maintenance.

But don't write off the idea. Picture a scenario in which a building owner, instead of purchasing an air-conditioning system, contracted with a provider for cooling. That provider, perhaps a manufacturer of air-conditioning equipment, would agree to cool the building to set levels in return for a monthly fee. It would be responsible for maintenance of the equipment and ultimately for its disposal. This scenario modifies a number of responsibilities and therefore incentives. It would be in the provider's interest to make equipment that lends itself to maintenance, repair, and upgrades, as well as future disassembly (since it's going to end up back in the provider's hands eventually).

Ownership vs. Product of Service: Air-Conditioning Example		
	Conventional Ownership	Product of Service Model
Construction Phase	Owner purchases all equipment and installation	Manufacturer provides equipment and installation
		⟶ Reduced or no upfront cost to owner
Occupancy Phase	Owner pays operating costs and maintenance/repairs	Owner pays service fee (lease) to manufacturer
		Manufacturer pays all operating/maintenance costs
		⟶ Manufacturer has incentive to design equipment to be more efficient,* durable, and repairable/upgradable
		*Assumes manufacturer also pays utility bill for operation of system
End of Life Phase	Owner has to dispose of equipment, including potentially toxic wastes	Manufacturer takes equipment back
		⟶ Manufacturer has incentive to design equipment to be disassembled and recyclable/reuseable

This table compares the benefits of products of service with the cost of conventional ownership of an air-conditioning system.

There are several green materials in this detail from a residential kitchen: the backsplash tiles and countertop are made of recycled glass; the blue panel is an EcoResin with 40 percent postindustrial recycled content; the cabinet veneer is FSC-certified; and the cabinet cores are made of wheatboard.

Now let's modify this contract so the air-conditioning provider also pays the electricity bill for the cooling. Suddenly, it's also in its interest to supply the most energy-efficient equipment feasible and to make the equipment upgradable as improved technologies become available. When tenants or owners are paying for electricity, they have a financial interest in efficiency but have less ability to upgrade and no involvement in the development of more efficient equipment. The shift in responsibilities, from owner to manufacturer, that occurs with products of service, has a potentially dramatic effect on the incentives for efficiency.

Social Responsibility and Materials

In "Ecodesign: What and Why," sustainability was defined to include social issues: how people and communities are affected. From a materials standpoint, this entails looking at aspects such as living wages, working conditions, child labor, and union rights. How are those bamboo farmers paid? Are those Tibetan rugs made by children? Is that overseas (or domestic, for that matter) factory a safe workplace? While you can't readily check these yourself, there are organizations like Fairtrade and GoodWeave (formerly RugMark) that certify social aspects of materials and products.[8]

Bear in mind that these materials criteria should not be looked at in isolation. Materials should be evaluated for multiple properties. Sometimes these properties (e.g., biobased and biodegradable) will dovetail, and sometimes they may conflict (e.g., biodegradable and durable). A new wallboard called EcoRock is one of the better examples of addressing multiple criteria. It is made largely from industrial waste materials (recycled content), has a low VOC content (nontoxic), is mold resistant (healthy), and requires much less energy to make than standard gypsum wallboard (energy efficient). A good question would be how you verify the claims made by the manufacturer—which leads us to the next chapter.

Labels and Ratings: Measuring Ecodesign

One of the legacies of both environmentalism and ecodesign, arising from their 1960s origins, is the perception that they are part of a touchy-feely tree-hugger movement with little science and objectivity behind them. At the same time, a confusing plethora of ecolabels and rating systems has evolved. It's tempting to say that we need to be able to separate the wheat from the chaff, but that phrase, which implies that the chaff is the useless stuff, would be misapplied here if taken literally. Chaff—the nonfood agricultural by-product of growing wheat—happens to be a useful material. As previously noted, we can make wheatboard from the industrial waste (a sort of preconsumer recycled content) that would otherwise be thrown away or burned.

There is, though, a kind of chaff to be challenged. In environmentalism in general and ecolabels in particular, we need to separate the greenwash from the truly green. We need to be able to evaluate choices and determine who to believe, as well as gauge how well we're doing. To do this, we'll look at labels and certifications for building materials and products, and then for the buildings themselves. We start with the material and product labels because understanding what they mean and how to use them is critical to the ecodesign process, but also because they set the stage for the more complex evaluation of buildings, which can be seen as a product of products.

Material and Product Labels

The chaff of ecolabels would be those that are inaccurate, not substantive, or untrustworthy. To be able to see through these requires knowledge of how the label is awarded and who is awarding it. It also requires knowing what exactly is being certified. To help clarify this, we can categorize labels in two ways: by the criteria and by the certifier.

On the criteria side, labels are divided into single-attribute and multiple-attribute. The chasing arrows recycling label is an example of the single-attribute type. It is based solely on whether the material has recycled content (though it is sometimes used—or abused—to indicate that a material is recyclable) and is unconcerned with other environmental issues. Similarly, Energy Star's only

	Single-Attribute	Multiple-Attribute
First Party/Self	♻ (ISO 14021 Type II)	"ENVIRONMENTALLY FRIENDLY" "ALL NATURAL"
Second Party/ Trade Organizations	GR+ PLUS	KCMA
Third Party/ Independent	FSC	EcoLogo (ISO 14024 Type I)
Environmental Product Declarations	SCS CERTIFIED 100% RECYCLED CONTENT	BEES 4.0 (ISO 14025 Type III)
User Based	Rate It Green™ Buy green confidently.	

Ecolabels should be evaluated in terms of who is supplying or verifying the data and what environmental criteria are being rated. Note that ISO 14024 Type I labels are multiple-attribute labels.

criterion is energy efficiency, and WaterSense evaluates only water efficiency. The Cradle to Cradle certification, on the other hand, looks at a whole range of environmental impacts, including energy and water efficiency, toxicity, and social responsibility. That makes it a multiple-attribute system.

Perhaps the bigger issue with ecolabels is the question of credibility. Faced with a seemingly exponential number of ecolabels, how do you know which ones to trust? To evaluate credibility, we can break down the labels into several categories, paralleling the types defined by ISO 14020.[1] A first-party label is a claim that is self-asserted, meaning that the company itself is the one making the assertion. The recycling label is a good example: there is no agency that oversees or owns that label; anyone can use it, and it goes largely unverified. Though a first-party claim may be accurate, it is hard to be sure, and so generally this is the least useful or trustworthy type of label.

A second-party label comes from an industry or trade organization. An example here is the Kitchen Cabinet Manufacturers Association's Environmental Stewardship Program certification. Because the program's requirements have been developed by the industry, rather than by an outside organization, a skeptic would question its independence from influence.

The label of the Sustainable Forestry Initiative (SFI) is perhaps another, though more complicated, example. The SFI label is marketed as an alternative to the Forest Stewardship Council (FSC) label. It was originally developed by a timber industry trade association and came under a lot of criticism for its lax requirements and lack of verification. It has subsequently evolved into a separate nonprofit organization, which now claims to have third-party verification. But many still doubt its independence and view its requirements as far weaker than FSC's.

The criteria for the FSC label, as with programs like Energy Star, WaterSense, and others, are developed by a third party that is separate from the manufacturer. Even here, though, one can assert a conflict of interest, in that some of these labels require the recipient to pay a (sometimes hefty) fee, on which the organization is often dependent.

True third-party labeling requires not only that environmental claims fulfill criteria set by an independent agency, but also that the claims be tested or verified by an independent party: either the labeling organization or an independent lab. Some organizations accept manufacturers' test results and claims in lieu of this testing or verification. When this is allowed, the credibility of the label is diminished and essentially means it is no longer a third-party, but really a second-party label.

Yet another category of labels is called Environmental Product Declarations. These are more like food nutrition labels or report cards: informational statements of the properties or impacts of a material or product, not necessarily assertions that they meet certain levels or criteria. If you see a Scientific Certification Systems (SCS) label declaring a percentage of recycled content, that means it has been tested and verified by SCS, in contrast to the better-known but unverified recycling symbol mentioned above.

Amid the seemingly constant announcement of new labels, ratings, and information sources, the collaboration between BuildingGreen.com's GreenSpec and the Healthy Building Network's Pharos Project, announced in 2010, may provide a one-stop shop for selection and evaluation of building materials. The subscription-based service combines and cross-references GreenSpec's reviews and vetted lists of green products with Pharos's transparent compilation of third-party ratings into an objective clearinghouse of environmental information with an extensive chemical and material library.

There is an informal fifth type of rating: user-based reviews. These are written by people who have used the product, much like the user reviews on Amazon or Epinions. Rate It Green (www.rateitgreen.com) is a site that posts green building product experiences and evaluations, enabling you to get real-world input. Pharos also includes a section for user reviews.

Life Cycle Analysis

The next part of understanding ecolabels is looking at the basis for their criteria and how the products are judged. The simplest designations use a checklist. More sophisticated processes, however, use life cycle analysis (LCA), also called life cycle assessment. Not to be confused with life cycle costing (LCC), LCA looks at all the inputs and outputs throughout the life of a material or product. What makes it different from LCC is that it gauges environmental and social impacts, as opposed to direct financial costs. The costs associated with these impacts frequently are not paid for by the manufacturer but are indirect societal costs. Climate change from greenhouse gas emissions is an obvious example: a fossil fuel power plant does not pay for the environmental toll resulting from its emissions. In economic jargon, this is an external cost, or externality. (Carbon taxes or cap-and-trade programs are supposed to address this particular externality by "internalizing" the cost of emitting carbon into the atmosphere.) Only when external charges are included do we know the true cost of something.

An LCA evaluates the stages of a product's life, typically starting with materials acquisition and continuing through fabrication, distribution, usage, and then to the product's end of life, whether that means a landfill or diversion to recycling. At each phase, there are material and resource inputs and resulting environmental impacts. The LCA process involves several steps, beginning with listing and quantifying the inputs, then multiplying the quantities by an ecological-impact factor or indicator that reflects the environmental toll per unit of each of the inputs. The difficulty is not in the multiplication, but in arriving at the relative impact factors of every material *and* the accompanying fabrication processes, as well as other life-cycle inputs like transportation or electricity consumption. What is the impact of a pound of steel relative to a pound of polystyrene or a kilowatt of electricity? And we need to know the end-of-life impacts for all the materials, too. What is the relative environmental effect of landfilling that steel versus recycling it? Developing these impact

The phases of a product's LCA.

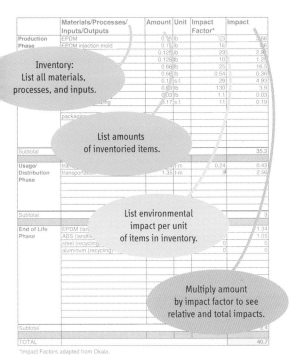

The steps in creating an LCA.

	INCANDESCENT		CFL		LED
	1 LAMP 1,000 HRS	40 LAMPS 40,000 HRS	1 LAMP 8,000 HRS	5 LAMPS 40,000 HRS	1 LAMP 40,000 HRS
PRODUCTION PHASE	·	●	·	●	●
USAGE PHASE	●	⬤	●	●	●
END OF LIFE	·	●	●	●	NA

Here is what a comparative LCA of incandescent, fluorescent, and LED light sources might look like, normalized for each source's life span. The size of each circle indicates the degree of impact.

factors and normalizing them with each other is a major task. Fortunately, there are databases and software applications available for this.

One of the problems with multiple-attribute evaluation is weighting. If the eco-impact factors take into account multiple types of environmental impacts, how is the relative importance of those impacts determined? How much weight is given to climate change versus water pollution versus indoor air quality? There is no single correct answer to this, since opinions vary on which environmental issues are most important. Some systems, such as LEED 2009, used extensive research to determine a consensus-based weighting. Less common are systems, such as Building for Environmental and Economic Sustainability (BEES), that let users determine their preferences.[2]

For practical purposes, LCAs are useful for comparing alternatives in building design. Light sources are a good example. In the lighting section of "Energy Efficiency: Active Techniques," the pros and cons of fluorescent lights were discussed. To make a fully informed choice between fluorescent and other sources, what is needed is an LCA comparing the true costs and impacts of incandescent, fluorescent, LED, and other lights. A study such as this would objectively compare the impacts throughout the life cycle of the products.

Creating an LCA of a product can be difficult enough. Now take it to the level of buildings. How do you perform an LCA for a construct as multifarious as a building, with its diversity of materials and products, as well as variables including location and users? This is a holy grail of sustainable building design, and there are a few programs working toward this goal. No tool is completely there yet, but BEES and the ATHENA Impact Estimator for Buildings are steps along the path.

Building Evaluation: LEED

Until we have a viable way to perform building LCAs, how do we evaluate our designs and our buildings? There are a few methods available, but the de facto standard for now has become the LEED rating system. The LEED program,

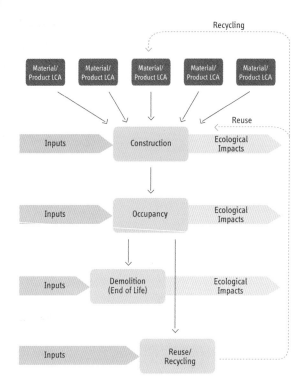

Recycling

| Material/ Product LCA | Material/ Product LCA | Material/ Product LCA | Material/ Product LCA | Material/ Product LCA |

Inputs → Construction → Ecological Impacts

Reuse

Inputs → Occupancy → Ecological Impacts

Inputs → Demolition (End of Life) → Ecological Impacts

Inputs → Reuse/ Recycling

In a building LCA, the completed, in-use phase of a building's life is usually referred to as the occupancy phase (rather than the usage phase in a product LCA). Buildings also have the added end-of-life possibility of renovation.

developed by the U.S. Green Building Council in 1998, has evolved considerably since its inception and is now in its third generation. In its most fundamental form, it is a checklist of ecodesign attributes for which points are awarded (some of the attributes are required).[3] The rating level a building achieves is determined by how many points it tallies. The checklist and points concept is both LEED's strength and weakness. As a checklist, it provides a relatively straight-forward path for the design team. But it has been criti-cized for devolving into more of a game in which racking up the most points sometimes takes precedence over pro-ducing the greenest building. These two goals may or may not coincide.

LEED has also been criticized for certifying projects almost as soon as they are completed. When this happens, there may be very little or no actual performance data and no knowledge of whether the building is working the way the models predicted or if users are operating its ecofea-tures as intended. In fact, some studies have indicated that a LEED-certified building may not be any more energy effi-cient than a conventional building.[4]

Of course, the way to avoid such doubt is to wait to certify a building until it has been through a period of usage or to require ongoing certification based on in-use performance. Some LEED categories are going the latter route with new requirements that certified buildings either follow up with certification under the Existing Buildings Operation and Maintenance category or file ongoing per-formance data (the updated version of LEED for Homes requires testing by a certified energy rater).

Building Evaluation: Other Certification Programs

The Living Building Challenge (LBC), on the other hand, takes the former route: requiring a performance testing period before the label can be awarded. This rating system has been developed by the Cascadia Region Green Building Council, which is a chapter of both the U.S. Green Building Council and the Canada Green Building Council serving the Pacific Northwest. The other aspect that differentiates the

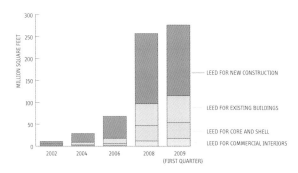

MILLION SQUARE FEET

LEED FOR NEW CONSTRUCTION

LEED FOR EXISTING BUILDINGS

LEED FOR CORE AND SHELL

LEED FOR COMMERCIAL INTERIORS

2002 2004 2006 2008 2009 (FIRST QUARTER)

Since 1998, the LEED rating system has expanded to include different types of buildings, neighborhood planning, and building operations (adapted from *Architectural Record*).

LBC from LEED (which it is meant to complement, not compete with) is that all of its checklist items are required for certification. There are no optional points. Combined with the one-year operations evaluation, the requirements make the LBC quite rigorous.

Another criticism of LEED is that the certification process can be very expensive and time consuming, particularly for small projects in which the administrative costs may be high relative to the overall budget. The National Association of Home Builders (NAHB) and International Code Council's National Green Building Standard (which replaced the NAHB's Model Green Home Building guidelines) and the Green Building Initiative's Green Globes system are in part responses to this issue. As with ecolabels, the fact that the guidelines were developed or heavily influenced by industry associations may lead some to question their validity. Conversely, others may claim that the involvement and input of many home-building and industry organizations make for more sensible rating systems.

Both Energy Star and WaterSense have moved beyond certifying just products and now have building certifications as well. WaterSense, at this point, has certification for homes only, while Energy Star has categories for homes and various types of commercial and manufacturing facilities. Like their product-labeling relatives, these are single-

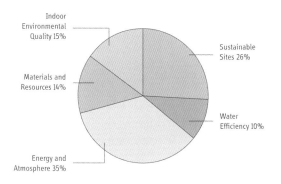

Indoor Environmental Quality 15%

Sustainable Sites 26%

Materials and Resources 14%

Water Efficiency 10%

Energy and Atmosphere 35%

Categories and allocation of points in LEED 2009. There are also ten bonus and innovation points, bringing the total to 110.

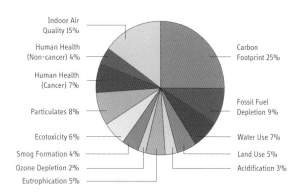

Indoor Air Quality 15%

Human Health (Non-cancer) 4%

Human Health (Cancer) 7%

Particulates 8%

Ecotoxicity 6%

Smog Formation 4%

Ozone Depletion 2%

Eutrophication 5%

Carbon Footprint 25%

Fossil Fuel Depletion 9%

Water Use 7%

Land Use 5%

Acidification 3%

LEED 2009 redistributed the points to place greater importance on climate change and carbon emissions (adapted from GreenSource).

Passive House (U.S.)
Requirements
Heating Demand: 15 kWh/m²/a (4,750 Btu/ft²/yr)
Cooling Demand: 15 kWh/m²/a (4,750 Btu/ft²/yr)
Total Primary Energy Demand (for heating, hot water, and electricity): 120 kWh/m²/a (38.1 kBtu/ft²/yr)
Air Leakage: 0.6 Air Changes per Hour @ 50 Pascal Pressure
Recommendations (varying with climate)
Window U-value: 0.8 W/m²/K (0.14 Btu/hr-ft²-°F) and 50% SHGC
Heat Recovery Ventilation System: 75% Efficiency and Electrical Consumption: 0.45 Wh/m³ (0.68 Wh/ft³)
Thermal Bridge-Free Construction with Transmittance: 0.01 W/m-K (0.006 Btu/hr-ft-°F)

Passive House requirements take a different approach than LEED, focusing on super-insulating the building's envelope in order to reduce the heating and cooling loads to near zero.

attribute certifications. They can be applied in conjunction with or separate from LEED ratings, as can the LBC.

There are a slew of other certifications out there, including EarthCraft and Passive House (mentioned in "Energy Efficiency: Passive Techniques"). For the moment, LEED is the closest to an industry standard. LEED will undoubtedly continue to evolve, as will other programs. The ideal system is holistic, flexible, responsive to local conditions, and not overly complex to administer.

We have a precedent for such a program in the form of food nutrition labels. While rating buildings is admittedly a far different endeavor, architects like Michelle Kaufmann have envisioned a "building nutrition label." It's more of a consumer awareness tool than a design tool, but a label like this could go a long way toward boosting awareness among both building users and those who design and construct buildings.

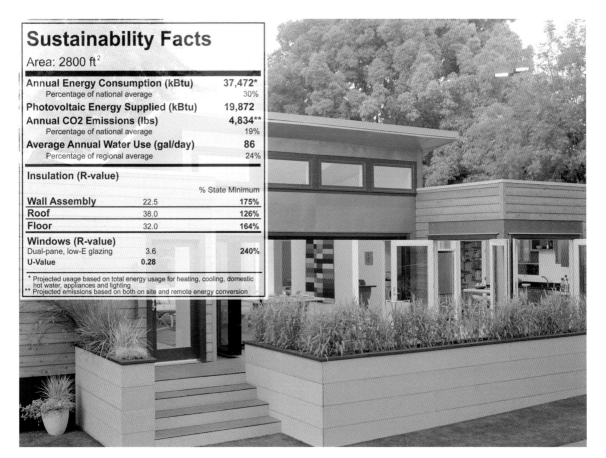

Sustainability Facts

Area: 2800 ft^2

Annual Energy Consumption (kBtu)		37,472*
Percentage of national average		30%
Photovoltaic Energy Supplied (kBtu)		19,872
Annual CO2 Emissions (lbs)		4,834**
Percentage of national average		19%
Average Annual Water Use (gal/day)		86
Percentage of regional average		24%

Insulation (R-value)

		% State Minimum
Wall Assembly	22.5	175%
Roof	38.0	126%
Floor	32.0	164%

Windows (R-value)

Dual-pane, low-E glazing	3.6	240%
U-Value	0.28	

* Projected usage based on total energy usage for heating, cooling, domestic hot water, appliances and lighting
** Projected emissions based on both on site and remote energy conversion

A nutrition label for homes as envisioned by Michelle Kaufmann.

The Future of Sustainable Design

The earliest forms of the built world, by necessity, were responsive to the environment and functioned in tandem with nature. In preindustrial days, people had no other choice. There was rudimentary heating and sometimes basic plumbing, but buildings were little more than shelters protecting their occupants from the extremes of the environment while working within what nature provided. Often these structures were natural and organic in the purest sense: they were made of tree limbs and thatch, skins, rocks, or ice. Then, when civilization advanced into the Industrial Revolution, the limitations fell aside and people could, by employing the harnessed brute force of machines, free themselves of the constraints imposed by local climates and local materials. In the main, this was a good thing: human conditions improved dramatically.

As we became more and more dependent on technological solutions and less reliant on nature, there was a dawning realization of the side effects—the drawbacks—of this newer dependency. Attempting to free ourselves from nature did not free us from consequences. In the second half of the twentieth century, a growing number of environmental issues, some actual, some potential, appeared. We became aware that the ironic outcome of loosening our dependence on nature might be the loss of those aspects of nature upon which our existence—or at the very least our lifestyles—necessarily depended.

At first, the reaction was to step backward to simpler buildings that were less energy driven. There were many exciting concepts and experiments, often combining new and old ideas. But for the most part, they were practiced far from the mainstream. The designs that resulted were usually not just a different aesthetic, but in-your-face different. The designs were alienated and alienating for most of the world of architecture, as well as for clients. It was alternative-lifestyle stuff, born of—or at least related to—the 1960s antiestablishment movements. There was no missing that it was green, even if it wasn't yet called that.

A lot of this architecture rejected technology, opting for passive designs made of used or natural materials, incorporating self-sufficient systems like rainwater harvesting,

Earthships, passive solar homes made from natural and recycled materials, are an example of early visible green design.

The Dynamic Tower concept by Dr. David Fisher is an example of incorporating high-tech solutions in a visible way. Each floor rotates separately, powered by wind turbines between the floors. The design also envisions that the building be entirely prefabricated, enabling rapid assembly.

and opting out of many of the modern conveniences the rest of us enjoyed. And in most cases, the structures were far from the urban and suburban regions where the majority of the U.S. population lived. However, when the oil shock of the 1970s struck, the interest in environmentalism and ecodesign became broader and the financial resources deeper. Thermal solar panels sprouted above our man-made landscapes, including, briefly, on the White House. Glazing technology improved. Mechanical equipment became more efficient. The ecodesign movement took on a new high-tech aesthetic, steeped in technology that was the solution rather than the problem.

One issue, though, was (and at times still is) the visible eco-aesthetic of the movement. There was a choice between being a Thoreau-like tree hugger living in the woods, and embracing the cutting edge of new technologies with designs that might look as different from a conventional building as an off-the-grid adobe hut. Eco-enthusiasts were categorized as hippies or geeks or possibly both, and that limited ecodesign's popular appeal.

In the 1980s and 1990s, a return to cheap energy took the wind out of the sails (and the sales) of energy efficiency. The real estate bubble gave rise to McMansions and monumental corporate buildings. Whatever efficiency improvements had been gleaned from the previous decades were vastly overwhelmed by the increase in materials and resources consumption generated by the sheer square footage of the boom.

But as the turn of the century heralded a reinvigorated interest in energy and environmental issues—spurred by once-again rising fuel prices as well as a growing acceptance and awareness of climate change—the perception and the implementation of ecodesign began to evolve. The schematic bases of the first earthy phase (passive solar design, essentially) were stripped of some of their alternative-lifestyle imagery and began to merge with technological solutions. This yielded idealized houses of the future (such as the Solar Decathlon entries) that Buckminster Fuller might have been proud of, as well as more-normal-looking prefabs and even spec buildings.[1] Corporate headquarters started to flaunt greenness, competing to see which tower or office park could rack up the most LEED points. This was, and remains, the beginning of the mainstreaming of ecodesign. It's an evolutionary step on the path from green design as an add-on, afterthought, or voluntary attribute to the integration of ecodesign as an inseparable part of design.

That integration has both process-related and aesthetic aspects. The process side is best exemplified in the integrated design approach described in "Ecodesign: What and Why," in which all parties to the project are brought together to brainstorm and to ensure everyone is on the same page. Integrated design also emphasizes that sustainability is at least as much at the core of the design process as other traditional design parameters like function and structure.

The aesthetic evolution is a little subtler but is crucial to the mainstreaming process. In order to shed the legacies of both organic and high-tech stereotypes and to merge green design into *all* of design, we must remove aesthetics from the equation and de-image ecodesign. Ecodesign becomes what I've been calling "transparent green."[2] The eco-aspects are still very much there; they just might not make themselves apparent, unless, of course, you're looking for them. When green design no longer connotes a look, it becomes less of a conscious choice, less of a statement, and less oriented toward a specific (and small) audience.

Transparent green designs may not be immediately identifiable as ecodesign.

This has pluses and minuses. The marketing thinking on hybrid cars for years had been that people didn't want to drive cars that looked different: the way to make fuel efficiency mainstream was to make the efficient cars look the same as regular cars. Comparing sales of the Prius, though, to sales of the hybrid Camry (which is indistinguishable from a conventional Camry) led to the conclusion that Prius sales were stronger because the buyers *wanted* people to know they were making an environmentally sound choice. What this tells us is that there are two types of buyers: a core group of people who are early adopters—like Prius owners, who will spend a bit more and want to make a statement—and another group who will "go green" only if it means *not* changing their lifestyles drastically and not standing out.[3] The same is true for buildings. There is a niche market for green "statement" architecture, but just as most of the world does not feel kinship with modern design (I was once told that 5 percent of furniture sales is modern and the rest is traditional), most do not want to stand out or change their habits.

So what is the best route to promoting green buildings and sustainability in general? Is it through educating people about consumption, so they desire—or better yet, demand—ecodesign? Or is it more effective to sneak it in, to practice what some of us call "stealth green"?

I believe this is a false choice; we can do both. Certainly the many aspects of ecodesign discussed here can be incorporated without affecting the look or even the budget of the project, and therefore they are fair game to include without necessarily involving the client. To *not* include them, arguably, is violating our professional responsibilities.

Other aspects, though, such as downsizing a residence following the *Not So Big House* principles, require us to educate our clients, to bring them willingly on board by helping them see what I've repeatedly called the win-win scenarios of ecodesign. We have to start by informing and educating ourselves, challenging old practices and assumptions when need be, so that we, in turn, can knowledgeably inform our clients. This shouldn't involve dragging them (or ourselves) along using the bitter-medicine argument. It needn't signify compromise from either a functional or aesthetic point of view. Rather, it's our role to find—to *design*—the solutions that deliver the best of all possible worlds: the ones that improve our lives now as well as those of future generations.

Before Rachel Carson, Buckminster Fuller, and Victor Papanek, to name just a few of the early visionaries, we had "design as usual": the Industrial Revolution "better living through chemistry" approach.[4] With growing environmental awareness, new approaches gained momentum on the fringes, becoming "green design as unusual." These were the initial "visible green" practitioners (predecessors to transparent green ones).

Science in Sight

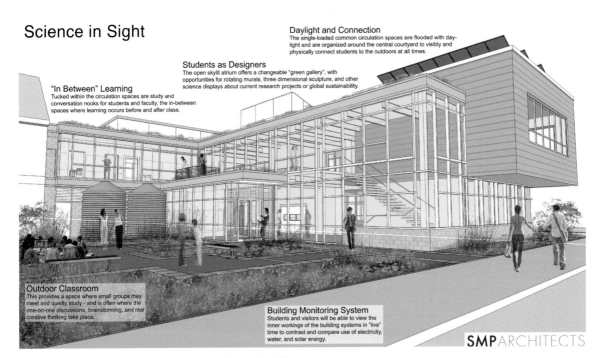

Daylight and Connection
The single-loaded common circulation spaces are flooded with daylight and are organized around the central courtyard to visibly and physically connect students to the outdoors at all times.

Students as Designers
The open skylit atrium offers a changeable "green gallery", with opportunities for rotating murals, three dimensional sculpture, and other science displays about current research projects or global sustainability.

"In Between" Learning
Tucked within the circulation spaces are study and conversation nooks for students and faculty, the in-between spaces where learning occurs before and after class.

Outdoor Classroom
This provides a space where small groups may meet and quietly study - and is often where the one-on-one discussions, brainstorming, and real creative thinking take place.

Building Monitoring System
Students and visitors will be able to view the inner workings of the building systems in "live" time to contrast and compare use of electricity, water, and solar energy.

SMPARCHITECTS

The potential problem with transparent green design is losing the ability to inform. The opposite approach might be called didactic visible green. In this design for a school, by SMP Architects, the architects chose to create "a building that teaches."

The phase we are entering now, with the general acceptance of environmentalism as a concern of the design world—and its adoption by regulation and code—is green design as usual, whether it's visible or transparent green and whether it comes at the client's request or the architect's urging or by stealth green.

The next stage, the ultimate realization of transparent green, will be a new version of design as usual: a design philosophy broadly adopted, perhaps even unspoken, that ecodesign is no longer optional, but is as integral a part of design responsibility as safety and as integral to design goals as aesthetics. Back in the first chapter, I discussed how green design should be considered just good design. I think we're on the verge of that ideal coming to fruition.

Also in that chapter, I described two approaches to greening design. The first is the tweak, the incremental step that diminishes the building's environmental impact. In contrast to the tweak is the innovation, the fundamentally new solution that can usually only result from changing the scale of the question being asked. It means changing the

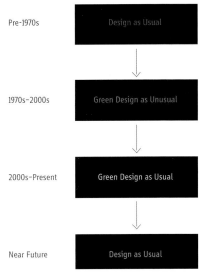

Pre-1970s — Design as Usual

1970s–2000s — Green Design as Unusual

2000s–Present — Green Design as Usual

Near Future — Design as Usual

The progression of design before eco awareness to design implicitly incorporating eco principles.

question, for instance, from "How do I reduce the energy load of a building?" to "How can I reconceive the building's concept so that it is not dependent on outside energy sources?" The first might involve CFLs and insulation, while the second might result in a Passive House or something entirely different, perhaps not yet imagined.

And maybe it will bring us full circle, back to architecture that is a part of nature, intertwined with and learning from the incredible efficiency and knowledge base that nature has created over the millennia. Buildings could emulate the environment with waste-free ecosystems. We see the beginnings of this in mundane areas like wastewater treatment and in more futuristic ideas such as the emerging three-dimensional printing techniques that may eventually allow us to construct our buildings additively—in essence to "grow" them. Or, we may literally grow buildings. Farfetched and fantastical perhaps, but there are truly organic buildings in the works, made of sprouting limbs instead of columns and beams.

As intriguing as it sounds, I doubt we'll be irrigating our columns, though we may be pruning our roofs. What we will undoubtedly end up with will be a mix of tweaks and innovations, of visible green and transparent green. There will be some green design as unusual to push our boundaries and a lot more stealth green design as usual. What is not in doubt is whether ecodesign will become an integral part of design—not an elective plaque on a building, but a perhaps invisible and matter-of-fact part of the design process.

Integrating nature in both the building and its construction, the Baubotanik Tower is a step in the utilization of mechanical, nonorganic materials to enable living plants to become actual structure. In this case, a temporary steel scaffold supports the plants until they reach the stage where the scaffold can be removed.

In the Fab Tree Hab, three MIT designers have proposed "a method to grow homes from native trees. A living structure is grafted into shape with prefabricated computer numeric controlled (CNC) reusable scaffolds . . . [enabling] dwellings to be fully integrated into an ecological community."

Endnotes

Ecodesign: What and Why

1. Christopher Hawthorne, "Turning Down the Global Thermostat," *Metropolis*, October 1, 2003, www.metropolismag.com/story/20031001/turning-down-the-global-thermostat.

2. It's important to differentiate life cycle analysis (LCA) from life cycle costing (LCC). LCC looks at the direct costs of something to its owner or user over its lifetime—purchase, supplies, maintenance, etc.—while LCA includes environmental and sometimes social costs. We'll discuss LCA in "Labels and Ratings: Measuring Ecodesign."

3. William McDonough and Michael Braungart, *Cradle to Cradle: Remaking the Way We Make Things* (New York: North Point Press, 2002); Buckminster Fuller, *Operating Manual for Spaceship Earth* (Carbondale, Ill.: Southern Illinois University Press, 1969). Fuller's book is also available online through the Buckminster Fuller Institute (www.bfi.org). It should also be noted that the Spaceship Earth concept predates Fuller and is referred to in, among other places, a 1966 essay by Kenneth E. Boulding, "The Economics of the Coming Spaceship Earth," in *Environmental Quality in a Growing Economy*, ed. Henry Jarrett (Baltimore: Johns Hopkins University Press, 1966), 3–14.

4. Biofuels rely on sunlight to grow. Tidal energy derives mostly from the moon's gravitational pull, and geothermal energy comes from the Earth's core; but they are generally grouped with renewable sources.

5. The triple bottom line concept is attributed to John Elkington in *Cannibals with Forks: The Triple Bottom Line of 21st Century Business* (Stony Creek, Conn.: New Society Publishers, 1998).

6. This is a bit of an oversimplification. Some business theories state that the only reason for a business's existence is to make money and external costs such as environmental impacts are irrelevant. But we're focusing on design, not business, and I think it's fair to say that our ethical responsibilities parallel the triple bottom line concept of economy, ecology, and equity.

7. Cynthia E. Smith, *Design for the Other 90%* (New York: Cooper-Hewitt, National Design Museum, with Editions Assouline, 2007). Exhibition catalog. *Design for the Other 90%* was an exhibition at the Cooper-Hewitt, National Design Museum that explored design for the 90 percent of the world's population who "have little or no access to most of the products and services many of us take for granted."

8. The committee is the World Commission on Environment and Development and is frequently referred to as the Brundtland Commission. The definition is contained in United Nations World Commission on Environment and Development, "Part II: Common Challenges," in *Our Common Future* (Oxford: Oxford University Press, 1987). The publication is also known as the Brundtland Report and can be found on the UN website (www.un-documents.net/ocf-02.htm).

9. Ibid. The original UN/Brundtland Report definition of sustainable development is "development that meets the needs of the present without compromising the ability of future generations to meet their own needs." But this definition is totally anthropogenic; nature is represented only insofar as it is necessary for human needs.

10. The concepts here derive from Abraham Maslow's hierarchy of needs, proposed in A.H. Maslow, "A Theory of Human Motivation," *Psychological Review* 50, no. 4 (1943): 370–96.

11. Salaries and benefits account for 85.8 percent of business operating costs according to the Light Right Consortium, as referenced in U.S. Environmental Protection Agency, "Chapter 6: Lighting," in *Energy Star Building Upgrade Manual* (Washington, DC: Energy Star, 2006), 7. This can be accessed on the Energy Star website (www.energystar.gov/index.cfm?c=business.bus_upgrade_manual).

12. Many people have advocated this. See Bruce Sterling, "What If Green Design Were Just Good Design?" *Dwell*, June 2001, 86–87.

13. As of this writing, the high energy prices of 2009 have retreated.

Site Issues

1. According to CNN.com, "between 1970 and 2000, the percentage of the total population living in suburbs grew from 38 percent to 50 percent." CNN.com, "U.S. Population Now 300 Million and Growing," October 17, 2006, http://www.cnn.com/2006/US/10/17/300.million.over/index.html.

2. Federal programs to make mortgages and home ownership more widely available fed this trend as well.

3. According to the Center for Sustainable Economy, an ecological footprint, or ecofootprint, is "the amount of land and ocean area required to sustain [an individual's or a region's] consumption patterns and absorb...waste on an annual basis." Urban footprints are almost always smaller than suburban or rural footprints due to the benefits of population density. Center for Sustainable Economy, www.myfootprint.org.

4. Congress for the New Urbanism is a nonprofit organization "promoting walkable, mixed-use neighborhood development, sustainable communities and healthier living conditions." "What Is CNU?," Congress for the New Urbanism, http://www.cnu.org/who_we_are.

5. To see the results of the competition, check out www.re-burbia.com. See also Ellen Dunham Jones and June Williamson, *Retrofitting Suburbia: Urban Design Solutions for Redesigning Suburbs* (Hoboken, N.J.: John Wiley & Sons, 2009), and Julia Christensen, *Big Box Reuse* (Cambridge, Mass.: MIT Press, 2008).

6. The organization Architecture 2030 has a very clear analysis of projected new construction and renovations in relation to the amount of existing square footage. "Solution: The Building Sector," Architecture 2030, www.architecture2030.org/the_solution/buildings_solution_how.

7. Biomimicry is the study of nature's systems, elements, and processes in order to emulate or take inspiration from them, specifically to solve human problems.

8. Kitta MacPherson, "From Top to Bottom, Butler Will Be a Living Environmental Laboratory," *News at Princeton*, August 13, 2009, http://www.princeton.edu/main/news/archive/S25/01/12M89/index.xml?section=featured. A study at Princeton University showed an almost 20°F (approximately 11°C) surface-temperature difference in June between a conventional roof (107°F) and a vegetated roof (88°F).

9. This barrier is being further broken down. Later in this book, in "The Future of Sustainable Design," there are illustrations of building concepts in which the buildings are actually grown.

Water Efficiency

1. U.S. Green Building Council, "Green Building by the Numbers," April 2009, www.USGBC.org/DisplayPage.aspx?CMSPageID=3340.

2. Rebecca Lindsey, "Looking for Lawns," NASA Earth Observatory, November 8, 2005, http://earthobservatory.nasa.gov/Features/Lawn/printall.php.

3. The state of Colorado partially ended its prohibition on rainwater harvesting in 2009. The restriction is based on state law regarding the ownership of water rights and is intended to protect downstream users.

4. There are rainwater capture systems that can provide drinking water, but they are less common in this country.

5. If the applicable plumbing code does not yet allow gray-water systems, consider installing the plumbing anyway with a bypass valve that can be switched when the code gets updated. (This is an example of futureproofing, discussed in "The Future of Sustainable Design.")

6. In response to the problems with early low-flow toilets, the Maximum Performance (MaP) tests, run by the California Urban Water Conservation Council, check the amount of solid matter that each toilet will successfully flush. California Urban Water Conservation Council, http://www.cuwcc.org/MaPTesting.aspx.

7. The terms *Eco-Machine* and *Living Machine* are sometimes used interchangeably to refer to this type of wastewater treatment system. The ecological designer John Todd was the first to call them Living Machines, but another company trademarked the term.

8. The term *sustainable development* has long been questioned as an oxymoron: how can we have any kind of long-term development without consuming resources? The answer can only be if that development does not engender consumption, that is, if it is self-sufficient or has a net-zero impact.

Energy Efficiency: Passive Techniques

1. U.S. Department of Energy, "Five Elements of Passive Solar Home Design," last updated September 14, 2010, www.energysavers.gov/your_home/designing_remodeling/index.cfm/mytopic=10270.

2. We assume northern-hemisphere orientations here. Reverse north and south for southern-hemisphere locations.

3. Enertia houses are designed and manufactured by Enertia Building Systems (www.enertia.com).

4. High-rise buildings almost invariably use metal frame windows or curtain walls.

5. Embodied energy will be discussed in "Materials."

6. LEED stands for Leadership in Energy and Environmental Design and is a building rating system that will be discussed more in "Labels and Ratings: Measuring Ecodesign."

7. Technically, hot air does not rise. Cold and therefore denser air falls, pulled by gravity, and displaces warmer air.

Energy Efficiency: Active Techniques

1. EERE, "Solar FAQs—Photovoltaics—The Basics," U.S. Department of Energy, http://apps1.eere.energy.gov/solar/cfm/faqs/third_level.cfm/name=Photovoltaics/cat=The Basics.

2. The National Renewable Energy Laboratory (NREL) has a free calculator called PVWatts. It is available at http://www.nrel.gov/rredc/pvwatts/version2.html. Others are offered by manufacturers. Examples can be found at the company websites of Sharp (http://sharpusa.cleanpowerestimator.com/sharpusa.htm) and RoofRay (http://roofray.com).

3. The Database of State Incentives for Renewables and Efficiency (DSIRE) can be found at http://www.dsireusa.org/.

4. Alex Wilson, "Putting Wind Turbines on Buildings Doesn't Make Sense," *BuildingGreen Blogs*, May 1, 2009, http://www.building-green.com/live/index.cfm/2009/5/1/Putting-wind-turbines-on-buildings-doesnt-make-sense; and Alex Wilson, "The Folly of Building-Integrated Wind," *Environmental Building News*, May 1, 2009, http://www.buildinggreen.com/auth/article.cfm/2009/4/29/The-Folly-of-Building-Integrated-Wind/.

5. Technically, *geothermal* refers to power plants that use deeper underground temperatures to generate electricity. To avoid confusion, *geoexchange* is the preferred term when discussing ground-source heat pumps.

6. Another method, underfloor air distribution (UFAD), is covered in the "Thermal Comfort" section of "Indoor Environmental Quality."

7. Patrick W. James et al., "Are Energy Savings Due to Ceiling Fans Just Hot Air?" Florida Solar Energy Center, August 1996, http://www.fsec.ucf.edu/en/publications/html/FSEC-PF-306-96.

8. Martin Holladay, "HRV or ERV?" *Musings of an Energy Nerd* (blog), GreenBuildingAdvisor.com, January 22, 2010, http://www.green-buildingadvisor.com/blogs/dept/musings/hrv-or-erv.

9. In the lighting industry, what we generally call bulbs are called "lamps"; lamps are called "fixtures"; and lights are called "luminaires."

10. The introduction of newer light sources has further complicated the use of color temperature and especially CRI as gauges. New gauges, such as color quality scale (CQS), are in development.

11. The EPA's recommendations for cleaning up a broken CFL can be found at http://www.epa.gov/cfl/cflcleanup.html.

12. David Bergman, "What's in a Name?" *Architectural Lighting*, March 2002, 40 (it can also be found at: http://www.archlighting.com/industry-news.asp?sectionID=0&articleID=452928). I wrote an article for *Architectural Lighting* several years ago proposing to change the name.

13. First observed by George E. Moore in 1965, Moore's law predicts the exponential increase in the processing power of computer chips. It roughly doubles every eighteen months. (The more accurate version is the doubling of the number of transistors on an integrated circuit every two years.)

14. Heschong Mahone Group, *Skylighting and Retail Sales: An Investigation into the Relationship between Daylight and Human Performance* (Fair Oaks, Calif.: Heschong Mahone Group, 1999); and Heschong Mahone Group, *Daylight and Retail Sales* (Fair Oaks, Calif.: Heschong Mahone Group, 2003).

15. Heschong Mahone Group, *Windows and Offices: A Study of Office Worker Performance and the Indoor Environment* (Fair Oaks, Calif.: Heschong Mahone Group, 2003); William McDonough and Michael Braungart, "Eco-Intelligence: The Anatomy of Transformation: Herman Miller's Journey to Sustainability with MBDC," *green@work*, April/March 2002, http://www.greenatworkmag.com/gwsubaccess/02marapr/eco. html; and Judith Heerwagen, "Sustainable Design Can Be an Asset to the Bottom Line," *ED+C*, July 15, 2002, www.edcmag.com/CDA/Archiv es/936335f1c9697010VgnVCM100000f932a8c0.

16. Bear in mind that cost-effectiveness may not be the only criterion. Regulation and altruism may also figure in.

Indoor Environmental Quality

1. Occupational Safety and Health Administration (OSHA), "Section III: Chapter 2: Indoor Air Quality Investigation," in *OSHA Technical Manual* (Washington, DC: U.S. Department of Labor, 1999), http://www.osha.gov/dts/osta/otm/otm_iii/otm_iii_2.html.

2. U.S. Environmental Protection Agency, "Indoor Air Facts No. 4 (revised) Sick Building Syndrome," last updated September 30, 2010, http://www.epa.gov/iaq/pubs/sbs.html. The EPA differentiates SBS from building-related illness (BRI), which is "when symptoms of diagnosable illness are identified and can be attributed directly to airborne building contaminants."

3. "Safety and Health Add Value...," OSHA, www.osha.gov/Publications/safety-health-addvalue.html.

4. Oddly enough, drug approvals take longer and are more difficult to obtain in the United States than in Europe, as manufacturers bear the burden of proof when demonstrating safety and efficacy.

5. Edward O. Wilson, *Biophilia* (Cambridge, Mass.: Harvard University Press, 1984).

Materials

1. "Building-related construction and demolition debris totals more than 136 million tons per year or nearly 40 percent of the C&D and municipal solid waste stream." U.S. Environmental Protection Agency, Region 5 Office of Pollution Prevention and Solid Waste, "What's in a Building: Composition Analysis of C&D Debris," Joint Project of the Santa Barbara County Solid Waste and Utilities Division, The Community Environmental Council, and the The Sustainability Project, http://www.epa.gov/reg5rcra/wptdiv/solidwaste/debris/brown fields/index.htm.

2. There have been a few promotional campaigns in which celebrities contributed their jeans or organized collections to make insulation, but the vast majority of the production is from postindustrial content.

3. In discussions on this topic, the conclusion has been that the only known type of materials upcycling is composting. The resulting soil is worth more than the waste it is made from, and the process requires minimal energy inputs. The counterpoint might be that we should be looking at recycling in terms of technical nutrients. Compostable waste is a biological nutrient.

4. The mercury content of the fly ash used in concrete is regulated.

5. Ecocertifications and labels are discussed in the next chapter.

6. Philip Proefrock, "Green Building Elements: Open Building," *Green Building Elements* (blog), April 30, 2007, http://greenbuildingele ments.com/2007/04/30/green-building-elements-open-build ing/#more-41.

7. Andrew Dey, "Reinventing the House," *Fine Homebuilding*, October/November 2006, 58–63.

8. The Fairtrade label is administered by Fairtrade Labelling Organizations International.

Labels and Ratings: Measuring Ecodesign

1. The ISO is the International Organization for Standardization, a nongovernmental organization that develops and publishes international standards. The ISO 14000 family addresses aspects of environmental management.

2. This issue is discussed in the section "Life Cycle Analysis."

3. LEED, it should be noted, does not certify or rate products or materials. Products and materials may help a building achieve points, but there is no such thing as a LEED-certified product.

4. Mireya Navarro, "Some Buildings Not Living Up to Green Label," *New York Times*, August 30, 2009; and Henry Gifford, "A Better Way to Rate Green Buildings," September 3, 2008, EnergySavingScience. com.

The Future of Sustainable Design

1. The Solar Decathlon is a biannual competition staged on the National Mall in Washington, DC, in which college teams construct energy-efficient prototype homes.

2. Transparent green has been the subject of many of my talks and was first discussed on the Sallan Foundation's website at http://www. sallan.org/Snapshot/2006/01/transparent_green_1.php.

3. Micheline Maynard, "Say 'Hybrid' and Many People Will Hear 'Prius,'" *New York Times*, July 4, 2007, http://www.nytimes.com/2007/07/04/business/04hybrid.html?ex=1341288000&en=4beada66541df849&e i=5124.

4. Rachel Carson is the author of *Silent Spring*, a seminal book that awakened a generation to some of the issues of synthetic chemicals and, by extension, technology in general. Victor Papanek, in *Design for the Real World* and other books, has spoken about the profession's responsibility to design for people's real needs.

Glossary

advanced framing: See *optimum value engineering*.

air exchanger: An advanced ventilation system used to aid outdoor-indoor air exchange between spaces and recover heating and/or cooling energy being exhausted. See also *energy recovery ventilator* and *heat recovery ventilator*.

amorphous silicon panels: See *thin-film panels*.

B

biobased: Made from living tissue. Usually refers to composites made from biomaterials (animal or vegetable) and/or from renewable materials.

biodegradable: Capable of being decomposed into innocuous materials by biological activity such as microorganisms.

biofuel: Fuel made from *biomass*.

biological nutrient: Material, usually organic, that can be safely reabsorbed into the environment and become the basis for another biological cycle. Compare *technical nutrient*.

biomass: An energy resource derived from organic matter such as wood, agricultural waste, or other living cell material.

biomimicry: The study of nature's systems, elements, and processes in order to emulate or take inspiration from them, specifically to solve human problems. Also called biomimetics.

biophilia: The theory that human beings have an innate tendency to interact with nature and its elements.

bioswale: Landscape element designed to remove silt and contaminants from surface runoff water.

biowall: See *vegetated roof (or wall)*.

black water: Wastewater that has come into contact with human, animal, or (sometimes) food waste. Contrast *gray water* and *white water*.

brise-soleil: An exterior sun-shading technique, usually using a horizontal surface or series of fins to block summer sun from windows.

brownfield: Land or buildings that have been developed, perhaps contaminated with hazardous substances, and then abandoned or underutilized, i.e., not virgin land. Contrast *greenfield*.

C

carbon footprint: A measure of the greenhouse gas emissions caused by an individual, group, or product. Usually measured in tons of CO_2 equivalent. Compare *ecological footprint*.

carbon neutral: The state of emitting no more carbon dioxide or greenhouse gases than are sequestered or offset. See also *net-zero energy/impact*.

chain of custody: Documentation of the stages of a material from acquisition to installation. Most often applied to a Forest Stewardship Council–certified material as it goes through the production process from the forest to the consumer, including all sequential stages.

chilled beam: A component for air-conditioning, enclosed in a beamlike construct, that uses water to remove heat from a room. Active chilled beams add fans to circulate the air.

chimney effect: See *stack effect*.

cluster housing/development: An area of dwellings grouped closely together in order to use the resulting land for open space, preservation, recreation, or agriculture.

color rendering index (CRI): A measure of how accurately a light source renders the color of objects compared to an ideal source. Zero is low and 100 is ideal. Compare *color temperature*.

color temperature: Also known as correlated color temperature (CCT). A measure of the whiteness of a light source, or how the light appears. Compare *color rendering index*.

constructed wetland: An artificial landscape created to treat water, mimicking the processes of natural wetlands.

cool roof: A roof having high reflectivity and high emissivity so that it does not heat up in summer, lowering both air-conditioning costs and *heat island* impact.

cradle to cradle (C2C): An approach to the design of systems, buildings, and materials that looks at the entire life cycle in the context of a closed loop of resources. Contrast *cradle to grave*.

cradle to grave: A linear view of an object's life span having a beginning (cradle) and an end (grave). Contrast *cradle to cradle*. See also *life cycle analysis*.

curtain wall: Outer, nonstructural covering of a building. Usually made primarily of glass.

D

dead mall: An underutilized or closed shopping mall.

dematerialization: In design usage, achieving the same or similar function with fewer (or no) material resources.

design for deconstruction: A design methodology that anticipates the end of life of a building or product, enabling the separation of materials for reuse, recycling, or decomposition. Compare *design for disassembly*.

design for disassembly (DfD): Similar to *design for deconstruction* but usually used in industrial design.

dew point: The temperature at which the air becomes saturated and cannot absorb additional moisture. When the dew point rises above the air temperature, water condenses, resulting in fog, dew, or precipitation. Warm air can hold more moisture. Therefore, as air is cooled (for example, by air-conditioning) and falls to temperatures nearer the dew point, it gets closer to saturation.

distributed power/generation: Decentralized or local power generation, such as onsite photovoltaic panels or wind turbines. Usually refers to power not connected to a distribution network (a.k.a. the grid).

downcycling: Recycling process in which the material loses value or quality.

E

earth-bermed/-sheltered: Built partially or wholly underground or with earth piled against it for insulating purposes.

ecological footprint: A measure of the land needed to support the existence of an individual or group. Often used to calculate how much land the entire human population needs or will need in the future relative to the amount of biologically productive land and sea area on the planet. Compare *carbon footprint*.

Eco-Machine: A system incorporating indoor tanks and/or constructed wetlands to clean water via natural processes.

efficacy: The capacity or power to produce an event. In the lighting industry, *efficacy* refers to the efficiency of the light source, or the amount of light output relative to energy consumed, often measured in lumens per watt (LPW).

embodied energy: The sum of all the energy used to extract, manufacture, ship, etc., a material, product, or building. Usually includes *feedstock energy* and sometimes energy used for end-of-life disposal.

energy recovery ventilator (ERV): A system used to transfer moisture as well as heat energy. See *air exchanger.* Contrast *heat recovery ventilator.*

Energy Star: Both a program and certification established by the U.S. Department of Energy in 1992 to achieve energy reduction in buildings and products.

environmental product declaration (EPD): A standardized statement of the environmental properties of a material or product, often incorporating *life cycle analysis* and defined in ISO 14020.

extensive green roof: A *vegetated roof* planted with shallow rooted vegetation, usually over a large area. Compare *intensive green roof.*

external cost (externality): A cost incurred by a third party, e.g., pollution costs not paid for by the polluter and therefore incurred by individuals or society.

F

feedstock energy: The energy used as an ingredient in producing a material, e.g., petroleum used as a material input (versus an energy source) in manufacturing plastics.

fly ash: A light ash residue from the burning of coal, generally required to be collected. Fly ash can be incorporated into concrete in place of energy-intensive Portland cement.

futureproofing: In design usage, the process of designing and constructing to anticipate future needs and developments, so that buildings and products do not become quickly outmoded technologically or functionally.

G

genetically modified organisms (GMO): Organisms whose genetic material (DNA) has been altered using genetic engineering.

geoexchange: One of the preferred terms (with *ground source* and *earth-coupled*) for geothermal heating so as to avoid confusion with geothermal power generation.

gray water: Wastewater from sinks, showers, kitchens, washers, etc. After purification, gray water is typically used for nonpotable purposes such as flushing and irrigation. Contrast *black water* and *white water.*

greenfield: Undeveloped land. Contrast *brownfield.*

green roof: See *vegetated roof (or wall).*

greenwashing: Employment of false or deceptive environmental claims. Marriage of "green" and "whitewashing."

H

heat island: An area, usually urban, in which air and surface temperatures are warmer due to greater heat absorption and diminished water evaporation of paved and built land.

heat pump: A device that moves heat from a cooler location to a warmer one. An air-source heat pump extracts heat energy from cold air and moves it to warm air. A ground-source, or geothermal, heat pump transfers heat between a building and the ground or a nearby water surface.

heat recovery ventilator: An air exchanger that allows transfer of heat between exhaust indoor air and outdoor fresh air. See *air exchanger.* Contrast *energy recovery ventilator.*

I

indoor air quality (IAQ): A measure of the amount of contaminants in the air of an indoor space. Compare *indoor environmental quality.*

indoor environmental quality (IEQ): A measure of the health and comfort of an indoor space, considering *indoor air quality* as well as temperature, humidity, and natural light.

insolation: A measure of the amount of solar radiation (direct and indirect sunlight) received on a surface. Used to estimate output of solar thermal or photovoltaic systems.

integrated design: A design method emphasizing collaboration of all involved parties (designers, owners, managers, consultants, etc.) early in the design process in order to promote a whole-building approach.

intensive green roof: A *vegetated roof* planted with deep-rooted vegetation, usually over a small area due to the weight.

L

LEED: Acronym for Leadership in Energy and Environmental Design. A green building rating system and professional accreditation. Buildings are rated as green (certified), silver, gold, and platinum (highest level of green).

life cycle analysis (LCA): An evaluation of the environmental impacts of a material, product, or building from *cradle to grave.* Also referred to as *life cycle assessment.*

light emitting diode (LED): A light source based on semiconductors, as opposed to heated filaments or charged gases. Also known as solid-state lighting (SSL). See also *organic light emitting diode.*

light pollution: Condition occurring when artificial light illuminates the night sky, often obscuring visibility of stars and indicative of energy waste.

light shelf: A horizontal surface adjacent to and usually near the top of a window to reflect light onto the ceiling, allowing natural light to reach deeper into a space.

light trespass: A form of *light pollution* in which unwanted light spills outdoors from one space to another.

livable street: Street which accommodates the needs of all users, not only automobiles. From the 1982 book of the same title by Donald Appleyard. Also referred to as *complete streets.* See also *walkable community.*

Living Building Challenge: A green building certification system originally developed by the Cascadia Green Building Council, now managed by the International Living Building Institute.

Living Machine: See *Eco-Machine*.

living wall: See *vegetated roof (or wall)*.

M

McMansion: A very large house, often pretentiously designed and/or poorly constructed.

N

natural: An unregulated term implying that a food or product does not contain synthetic materials and/or does not use pesticides, synthetic fertilizers, etc. See also *organic*.

negawatt: A negative megawatt, as in power that does not need to be produced because of energy efficiency or conservation. Coined by Amory Lovins.

net metering: Used when onsite power generation is combined with the power grid. When a building is generating more power than it is using, then the electric meter runs backward, indicating that power is, in effect, being sold to the power company.

net-zero energy/impact: State of producing as much energy as is used on an annual basis. May include additional environmental categories such as water. See also *carbon neutral*.

New Urbanism: A community design approach emphasizing town or urban characteristics of walkability, mixed use, and high density. Codified by the Congress for the New Urbanism. See also *smart growth* and *walkable community*.

O

off-gassing: Emission of noxious chemicals or gases from a material at normal atmospheric pressure.

off-the-grid: In general, existing self-sufficiently without dependence on outside support. For buildings, operating without being connected to public utilities (electricity, gas, water, sewage treatment).

on-demand water heater: A device to make hot water when needed. Contrast to hot water tanks, which maintain heated water ready for use.

open building: An approach to design and construction that views buildings as made of multiple layers distinct from one another but coordinated, so that elements of the building can be upgraded or modified nondestructively.

optimum value engineering: Construction design that maximizes efficient use of materials without compromising strength, usually in reference to wood framing. Also called *advanced framing* design or *advanced framing* techniques.

organic: When used in reference to foods and certain other products, defined by the U.S. Department of Agriculture to mean "produced by farmers who emphasize the use of renewable resources and the conservation of soil and water to enhance environmental quality for future generations." The USDA has established three levels of organic certification. See also *natural*.

organic light emitting diode (OLED): A type of *light emitting diode* utilizing a thin film of organic compounds rather than the point-source silicon-based light sources in LEDs. See also *light emitting diode*.

P

Passive House: A design approach and certification for energy-efficient buildings.

photovoltaic cell: A device that converts sunlight directly into electricity. Photovoltaic (PV) cells are silicon-based semiconductors and are often referred to as *solar cells*.

photovoltaic panel: An assembly of solar cells that converts sunlight (solar radiation) to electricity. See *photovoltaic cell*.

postconsumer recycling: Reprocessing of materials or products that have previously completed a life cycle as a consumer item.

postindustrial recycling: Reprocessing of materials generated during manufacturing processes, usually scrap material, that have not been used in consumer products.

precautionary principle: An approach to environmental regulation that involves acting to avoid serious or potential harm to health or the environment despite lack of scientific certainty.

preconsumer recycling: See *postindustrial recycling*.

products of service: Process of offering the service of a product as opposed to the ownership of it. Since ownership of the product remains with the manufacturer (or service provider), incentives for repairing and recycling and sometimes for upgrading are shifted to the manufacturer, enabling closed loop systems. Products of service may also have a business advantage over conventional products of consumption.

Q

qanat: An underground aqueduct system to convey water by gravity from highlands. Developed in ancient Persia 2,500–3,000 years ago.

R

radiant barrier: A layer of material, usually reflective, that inhibits radiant transfer of heat. Often used in attics.

radiant heating: System in which the heat is emitted by radiation, as opposed to convection, from a warmed material. The most common methods are hydronic systems, which circulate hot water in tubes, or electric systems, which utilize heating elements under or in the floor.

regenerative design: An approach to ecodesign that goes beyond sustainability to repair, or regenerate, natural systems.

retention pond or basin: A permanent artificial pool of water created to manage stormwater runoff.

R-value: A unit of thermal resistance. See also *U-value*.

S

sick building syndrome: Medical conditions or discomfort experienced by building occupants that appear to be caused by exposure to indoor pollutants. Occupants experience relief of symptoms shortly after leaving the building. Different from building-related illness, in which the symptoms are diagnosed and the contaminant identified.

smart grid: Update of the electric grid (or net) to accommodate two-way information transmission. Enables energy-efficient advances such as use of off-peak power for smart appliances and net metering for onsite power generation.

smart growth: Related to *New Urbanism*, a planning concept to counter the effects of sprawl.

solar chimney: A vertical shaft that naturally ventilates a building as passively heated air rises through it, creating negative pressure below. Also called *thermal chimney*.

solar/thermal collector: System to gather solar radiation to heat a thermal storage material, usually water. *Photovoltaic panels* may be considered a form of solar collector but are usually categorized separately.

stack effect: The movement of air through a space by making use of temperature differentials, i.e., hot air rising. Also called *chimney effect*.

structural insulated panels (SIP): A composite construction material in which rigid foam insulation is sheathed with a skin. Usually made of oriented strand board (OSP).

swale: A shallow land depression that diverts or directs water runoff. See also *bioswale*.

T

technical nutrient: Material, often synthetic, that is safe for the environment and can be continuously reused in a closed-loop cycle. Compare *biological nutrient*.

thermal bridge: Route through which heat can travel more easily between two materials, usually via a material with high thermal conductivity, such as metal.

thermal energy storage: Method of energy storage, usually involving use of off-peak power to make ice or chilled water for later use during peak power periods.

thermal mass: Any mass that can absorb heat. Materials with high thermal mass can absorb larger amounts of heat and then release it gradually, balancing out the hot and cold cycles of a day. See also *Trombe wall*.

thin-film panels/cells: Device to generate electricity from panels made of thin layers of film (as opposed to the more conventional silicon *photovoltaic panels*).

three Rs: *Reduce*, *reuse*, and *recycle*—the early mantra of the ecology movement. The three strategies are in hierarchical order of importance. Various fourth Rs, such as *rethink* and *recovery*, are sometimes added.

triple bottom line: An expansion upon conventional bottom-line accounting to include *external costs* to the environment and society. The three bottom lines are often referred to as *people, planet, and profit* or *economy, ecology, and equity*.

Trombe wall: A passive heating system consisting of a south-facing vertical wall with high *thermal mass*, an air space, and a translucent surface through which solar energy passes and is absorbed by the wall. Named for Felix Trombe, who popularized (but did not invent) the concept.

U

upcycling: Recycling process in which the resulting material or product has more value or better quality. The laws of thermodynamics would seem to indicate that upcycling of materials, strictly speaking, is not possible.

U-value: The mathematical inverse of *R-value*. Usually used in reference to the thermal value of windows.

V

vegetated roof (or wall): A roof (or wall) of a structure that is covered at least in part by vegetation. A vegetated roof is made of several layers including a growing medium and a root barrier on top of a waterproof membrane (which may be a conventional roof). Similarly, vegetated walls, or living walls, are composed of the actual wall along with either planters or vines to train vegetation on the outside. There are also indoor versions of living walls. See also *extensive green roof* and *intensive green roof*.

vertical garden: Structure for agriculture in high-rise urban structures, or a *vegetated wall* devoted to edible plants.

volatile organic compound (VOC): An organic compound that evaporates at room temperature and is often hazardous to human health, causing poor indoor air quality.

W

walkable community: A community designed around residences and goods and services within walking, bicycling, or other nonautomobile means of transportation. See also *New Urbanism*.

WaterSense: An ecolabel developed by the U.S. EPA to promote water-efficient products.

white water: Potable (drinkable) water. Contrast *black water* and *gray water*.

X

xeriscape: Landscape method using materials and vegetation that reduce or eliminate the need for irrigation, especially in arid climates.

Resources

Birkeland, Janis. *Design for Sustainability: A Sourcebook of Integrated, Eco-Logical Solutions*. London: Earthscan, 2002.

Dunham-Jones, Ellen, and June Williamson. *Retrofitting Suburbia: Urban Design Solutions for Redesigning Suburbs*. Hoboken, NJ: Wiley, 2009.

Ginsberg, Gary, and Brian Toal. *What's Toxic, What's Not*. New York: Berkley, 2006.

Gissen, David, ed. *Big & Green: Toward Sustainable Architecture in the 21st Century*. New York: Princeton Architectural Press, 2003.

Johnston, David, and Scott Gibson. *Green from the Ground Up: Sustainable, Healthy, and Energy-Efficient Home Construction*. Newtown, CT: Taunton, 2008.

Mazria, Edward. *The Passive Solar Energy Book: A Complete Guide to Passive Solar Home, Greenhouse, and Building Design*. Emmaus, PA: Rodale, 1979.

McDonough, William, and Michael Braungart. *Cradle to Cradle: Remaking the Way We Make Things*. New York: North Point Press, 2002.

McLennan, Jason F. *The Philosophy of Sustainable Design: The Future of Architecture*. Kansas City, MO: Ecotone, 2004.

Susanka, Sarah, and Kira Obolensky. *The Not So Big House: A Blueprint for the Way We Really Live*. Newtown, CT: Taunton Press, 2001.

Yeang, Ken. *Ecodesign: A Manual for Ecological Design*. London: Wiley-Academy, 2006.

Yudelson, Jerry. *Green Building A to Z: Understanding the Language of Green Building*. Gabriola Island, BC: New Society, 2007.

BuildingGreen. www.buildinggreen.com

Building Science Corporation. www.buildingscience.com

Green Building Advisor. www.greenbuildingadvisor.com

Oikos. http://oikos.com

Passive House Institute U.S. www.passivehouse.us

The Pharos Project. www.pharosproject.net

U.S. Department of Energy. www.eere.energy.gov

U.S. Green Building Council: Research Publications. www.usgbc.org

Credits

All photographs by David Bergman or Lori Greenberg unless otherwise indicated. All illustrations and charts by Lori Greenberg and Jason Q. Bailey unless otherwise indicated.

11t: Courtesy, The Estate of R. Buckminster Fuller; 11b: Adapted from "Gross Production vs. Genuine Progress, 1950–2004," Redefining Progress, Oakland, CA, www.rprogress.org; 12: CPG Consultants; 15: Adapted from USGBC; 18: Courtesy, The Estate of R. Buckminster Fuller; 20b: Purnima McCutcheon/Architecture for Humanity; 22t: D'Arcy Norman; 22b: James Corner Field Operations; 23: Vincent Callebaut Architectures; 24: Adapted from Construction Users Roundtable, "Collaboration, Integrated Information, and the Project Lifecycle in Building Design and Construction and Operation" (WP-1202), August 2004; 25: Adapted from greenandsave.com; 30t: Southeastern Wisconsin Regional Planning Commission; 30bl: ©iStockphoto.com/NLN; 30br: ©iStockphoto.com/ toddmedia; 31: Michael Mehaffy; 32: Courtesy of Bing Thom Architects; 33t: Adapted from National Association of Home Builders, "(Housing Facts Figures and Trends for 2006"; 33b: Courtesy of Susanka Studios; 34t: Courtesy of American Hydrotech, Inc.; 34b: © Cook+Fox Architects; 35t: Courtesy of Bomonite; 35b: Environmental Design & Construction, "Green Roofs: Stormwater Management from the Top Down," January 15, 2001; 36t: Courtesy of Little Diversified Architectural Consulting; 36bl: Patrick Blanc; 36br: Courtesy of the Vertical Farm project; 37: Doug Klembara; 39t: Adapted from USGS, "Earth's Water Distribution"; 39b: Adapted from U.S. EPA, "Indoor Water Use in the United States"; 40tl: Leslie Furlong; 40tr: Photo by Fritz Haeg; 42t: © 2009 John Todd Ecological Design/J.C. Bouvier; 42bl/br: © Anne Mandelbaum; 43: Svr Design Company; 46t/b: Chandler Lee; 47t: Adapted from DOE, "Passive Solar Design for the Home," February 2001; 50tl/tr: Alexis Kraft; 50bl/ br: Adapted from LBNL; 51: Adapted from Enertia.com; 52t: Photo by Brad Feinknopf; 52bl/br: Photo by Michele Alassio; 53t: Bull Stockwell Allen, Architecture + Planning; 55: Courtesy of The National Fenestration Rating Council (NFRC); 61t: © Anne Mandelbaum; 62m: Adapted from worldarab.net; 62t: Perry L. Aragon; 62bl: Nigel Paine; 63l: Image courtesy of City of Melbourne; 63r: Nick Carson at en.wikipedia; 64t: KPF; 64b: H.G. Esch; 65: Jeremy Wold; 68bl/br: Adapted from southface. org and homepower.com; 69t: SunMaxx; 69b: SRG Partnership, Inc.; 71t: Courtesy of Global Solar Energy, Inc.; 71m: Evo Energy; 71b: SRG Partnership, Inc.; 72t: Architect: Oppenheim Architecture + Design; Renderings: Dbox; 72b: Quietrevolution; 73: Provided courtesy of HOK/ credit: Steve Hall of Hedrich Blessing; 74: Adapted from DOE/EERE; 76tl/ tr: Adapted from buildinggreen.com; 76b: Warmboard Radiant Subfloor; 77: Adapted from iaqsource.com; 81: Author's collection; 83: Adapted from U.S. EPA; 86: Adapted from energystar.gov; 87tl: David Bergman Architect; fixture from Bruck; 87tr: Philips Lighting; 87b: Courtesy of Lutron Electronics Co., Inc.; 88: Agilewaves; 89t: Architectural Grilles and Sunshades, Inc. (AGS, Inc.); 89b: Image courtesy of Parans Solar Lighting; 90: Autodesk and Integrated Environmental Solutions Limited; 91: Adrian Smith + Gordon Gill Architecture; 93: Adapted from OSHA Technical Manual; 95: David Bergman Architect; 98l/r: Photos by Enrico Cano; 101: Adapted from NAHB, "Residential Construction Waste: From Disposal to Management"; 102t: Gregg Eldred; 102b: Courtesy, The Estate of R. Buckminster Fuller; 103t: Benny Chan; 103b: Garrison Architects; 104tl: Energy Panel Structures, Inc.; 104tr: Image courtesy of FLIR Systems; 104b: EHDD Architecture; 105: Nigel Young / Foster + Partners; 106b: Coverings, Etc.; 107t: David Bergman Architect; 107b: Adapted from Architecture 2030, "Material Selection and Embodied Energy," www.architecture2030.org/regional_solutions/materials.html; 109t/b: Dreamstime; 110: From the Collections of The Henry Ford; 112t: Herman Miller; 113t: Photo by Gregory La Vardera Architect; 113b: Photo by Gregory La Vardera Architect; 118: All logos used by permission. FSC Trademark © 1996 Forest Stewardship Council A.C.; 121b: Sources: Deanna H. Matthews, et. al., "DOE Solid-State Lighting Life Cycle Assessment," Green Design Institute, Carnegie Mellon University, 2009; Osram, "Life Cycle Assessment of Illuminants: A Comparison of Light Bulbs, Compact Fluorescent Lamps and LED Lamps," November 2009; Laurie Ramroth, "Comparison of Life-Cycle Analyses of Compact Fluorescent and Incandescent Lamps Based on Rated Life of Compact Fluorescent Lamp," Rocky Mountain Institute, February 2008; and Maarten ten Houten, "LCA and Green Product Design"; 123t: Adapted from Architectural Record, May 2009; 123br: Adapted from GreenSource, "Building a New LEED," November 2008; 125: Designs by Michelle Kaufmann; photo by John Swain Photography; 128t: Ron Guillen; 128b: All rights are reserved to Dr. David Fisher and related to Dynamic Architecture; 130: David Bergman Architect; 132: SMP Architects; 134: ©Ferdinand Ludwig, IGMA/ University of Stuttgart; 135: Dr. Mitchell Joachim, Terreform ONE